# Gluten-Free, High Protein, *Mostly* Vegetarian Recipes & Cookbook

## Simple, Tasty Meals, 30 Minutes or Less

*by*

### Bo Sebastian

Copyright © 2014
All rights reserved.

Bo Sebastian

Finding Authentic You Publishing
Copyright © 2014 by Bo Sebastian
Printed in the United States of America.
All rights reserved. No part of this book may be reproduced in any form or by any electronic or mechanical means, including information storage and retrieval systems, without permission in writing from the publisher, except by a reviewer, who may quote brief passages in a review.
We here at F. A. You Publishing enjoy hearing from readers. You can e-mail us at:
editor@findingauthenticyoupublishing.com
Visit our other websites:
http://www.FindingAuthenticYouPublishing.com
Author's Website: http://www.BoSebastian.com
Blog: http://www.FindingAuthenticyou.com

10 9 8 7 6 5 4 3 2
Cover Design: Bo Sebastian
Interior Design: Bo Sebastian

Gluten-Free, High-Protein, Vegetarian Cookbook

# TABLE OF CONTENTS

Introduction ................................................................. 7

Chapter One: The Vegetarian Protein Palate ................... 9

    Basic Recipe: Baked Tofu ............................................... 13

    Recipe: Fried Tofu ........................................................ 13

Chapter Two: Herbs, Spices, and Thickening Agents .. 17

Chapter Three: Other Food Enhancements ................... 20

Chapter Four: Cooking with Inspiration ....................... 24

    Recipe: Basic Broth ...................................................... 25

    Recipe: Vinaigrette ...................................................... 27

Chapter Five: Breakfast .................................................. 31

    Recipe: Protein-Fortified Oatmeal ............................... 31

    Recipe: Breakfast—Steel-Cut Oats ............................... 32

    Recipe: Breakfast—Scrambled Tofu or Egg Substitute ..................................................................... 32

    Recipe: Weight Loss: Berries and Yogurt ................... 33

    Recipe: Gluten-Free Pancakes ..................................... 33

Chapter Six: Snacks ........................................................ 34

    Recipe: Snack—Hummus ............................................ 36

Chapter Seven: Dinner and Lunch Recipes ................... 38

NORTH AMERICAN DISHES ........................................ 40

    Recipe: Complete Meal—Tiger Food .......................... 40

    Recipe: Lunch Meal—Barbecue Vegetable Roll-ups ....................................................................... 42

    Recipe: Dinner Meal—Chicken-Style Stroganoff ..... 43

    Recipe: Quick Meal—Veggie Burgers, Sweet Potato

Fries, and Salad. ............................................................. 45

Recipe: Meal—Kale Stew with Quorn Nuggets ........ 46

Recipe: Main Course Protein—
Barbecued Tempeh ........................................................ 48

Recipe: Side Dish—Stuffed Yellow Squash ............... 49

Recipe: Side Dish—Stuffed Zucchini Squash with
Protein .............................................................................. 51

Recipe: Meal—Tofu, Herb Vegetable Soup ............... 53

Recipe: Main Course Protein— Tofu Burgers .......... 55

Recipe: Side Dish—Skillet Fried Potatoes with
Rosemary ......................................................................... 57

Recipe: Dressing—Shitake Sesame ............................ 58

Recipe: Main Course— Basic Bean Recipe ............... 59

Recipe: Main Course—Cuban Black Beans .............. 61

Recipe: Condiment—Fresh Salsa ............................... 63

Recipe: Meal—Salad with Chik'n or Baked Tofu ..... 64

Recipe: Meal—Yeast Gulch Gravy & Buddha Bowl . 65

Recipe: Side Dish—Rosemary Mashed Potatoes ..... 66

Recipe: Side Dish—Marinated Roasted
Vegetables ....................................................................... 67

Recipe: 10-Minutes Meal—Vegetarian Reuben
Sandwich ......................................................................... 68

Recipe: Side Dish—Tofu Au Gratin ............................ 69

**JAPANESE DISHES** ............................................................ 70

Recipe: Dressing—Miso-Carrot ................................... 70

Recipe: Appetizer—Miso Soup .................................... 71

Recipe: Side Dish—Cold Szechwan
Sesame Noodles ............................................................. 72

Recipe: Main Course Protein—Teriyaki Tofu .......... 74

Recipe: Meal—Greenwich Village Favorite ............. 75

**ITALIAN DISHES** ................................................................. 76

Recipe: Appetizer—Agli a Olia Soup ...................... 76

Recipe: Main Protein—Baked Italian-Style Tofu .... 78

Recipe: Sauces—Fresh Tomato Sauce ..................... 80

Recipe: Sauce—Sun-Dried Tomato Pesto ............... 82

Recipe: Sauce—Sweet Basil Pesto ........................... 84

Recipe: Main Course Protein—Italian Soysage
and Fried Peppers ................................................... 85

Recipe: Quick Meal—Pizzazzing a Gluten-Free
Pizza ........................................................................ 86

Recipe: Hearty Soup—Pasta y Faziole .................... 87

Recipe: Main Course— Cold Pasta Salad ................ 88

Recipe: Main Course Protein—
Stuffed Bell Peppers ............................................... 90

**MEDITERRANEAN FARE** ................................................ 91

Recipe: Appetizer—Lentil Soup .............................. 91

Recipe: Dressing—Cucumber Yogurt Dressing ...... 92

Recipe: Side Dish—Tabouli ..................................... 93

Recipe: Protein Main Dish—Falafel ........................ 94

Recipe: Main Course Protein—
Fried Marinated Greek Tofu ................................... 96

Recipe: 10-Minute Meal—Tofu Salad ..................... 97

**CHINESE (ASIAN) DISHES** ............................................. 98

Recipe: Soup—Hot and Sour Soup ......................... 98

Recipe: Soup—Vegetable-Tofu Soup .................... 100

Recipe: 10-Minute Meal— Egg Foo Yong ............. 101

**Recipe: Main Course—Stir-Fried Vegetables..........103**

**Recipe: Main Dish—Lomein Substitute ....................106**

**Recipe: Main Course Protein—Kung Pao Tofu......107**

**Other Health Tips ................................................................108**

Gluten-Free, High-Protein, Vegetarian Cookbook

# Introduction

Becoming a vegetarian is a big leap for most people after eating meat their entire lives. Then, after much reading and exploration, you discover that gluten is the major problem with IBS (Irritable Bowel Syndrom) and also causes brain disorientation, and arthritic pain. What, then, is safe to eat? Almost every vegetarian item has either soy or wheat gluten in its contents.

I had been a vegetarian for 17 years- vegan for some of that time. At first, the challenge was mostly to modify the protein supplements to taste like meat. In my first cookbook, *The Protein-Powered Vegetarian*, the protein substances I used were mostly tofu- and seitan-based, the latter causing the most irritation for people with wheat sensitivity. Physician after physician firmly suggested to me that my vegetarian clients with IBS should go back to eating meat. Some vegetarians with severe IBS and Celiac Disease were whithering away, because of so much stomach upset. Everything they ate quickly sent them running to the bathroom.

If you have IBS or know someone who has it, you know that eating can be a challenge. Once you discover what you can actually consume, you realize that simple carbs are the highest in the food groups that cause the least amount of digestive problems. So, what is left to do but eat pasta and bread until you become bloated and overweight.

Obesity is a huge problem in the world today! The solution to this problem could be a gluten-free diet. When I took the gluten out of my own and client's diets, all of us immediately began to see signs of relief with weight gain and arthritis, even the IBS. We had more energy. We were able to eat more vegetables without stomach upset. We felt as if our bodies let go of a heavy weight, as muscles began to become supple again.

Personally, I'm a yogi. So, for years I have gingerly rolled out of bed and on to the floor, because sleeping caused such back and hip problems, as an arthritic condition does. Within a month of going gluten free, I had begun to get back to my health from twenty years ago. I get right out of bed now and do a yoga practice that is worthy of being called a practice. I can easily put my palms to the floor as I bend over. I had decreased the fat content of my body from 29.8% to 13.9% in a mere three months.

Here are some recipes I used to keep me gluten free and energy packed with protein and remain an *almost* vegetarian. (I'll explain the "almost" a little later.)

Gluten-Free, High-Protein, Vegetarian Cookbook

# Chapter One:
# The Vegetarian Protein Palate

Let's start with the food that is rich in protein, because most people begin here to create meals. As I said in the introduction, most vegetarian, meat-free products contain gluten. So, finding vegetarian products that are gluten free is our first task.

### Quorn™ Products

I love this company. I especially enjoy using the Quorn Pieces and Quorn Chicken-Style Roast. But, you'll have to choose if you want to take a chance at a hint of gluten. Remember: even oatmeal, which is completely gluten free could contain contaminants from the processing factory. So, most companies are afraid of lawsuits, because of cross-contamination. Personally, I don't have Celiac Disease, so I'm not afraid of a miniscule amount of wheat.

According to a letter that the company will send you, if you take the time to inquire if Quorn™ products are gluten free, here is what you'll receive:

*Firstly, according to our suppliers, the following Quorn products do not contain added gluten:*

*Quorn Pieces (chilled and frozen)/Quorn Plain Fillets (chilled and frozen)/Quorn Chicken Style Roast (frozen)/Quorn Deli Chicken Style (chilled) Quorn Deli Wafer Thin Chicken Style (chilled) Quorn Deli Roast Chicken Style (chilled) Quorn Deli Ham Style (chilled)/Quorn Deli Smokey Ham Style (chilled)/Quorn Deli Bacon Style (chilled)/Quorn bacon/ rashers (frozen)/Fajita strips.*

*However, in the light of recent amends to Labeling Legislation regarding the indication of the presence of allergens in food products, (this includes 14 food ingredients), Marlow Foods have completed a thorough assessment of our manufacturing process.*

*As a result of this assessment, we have made the decision that, where we handle gluten-containing products in our factories, we will not recommend these products as suitable for a gluten-free diet, even though gluten is not included in the recipe. Although we have taken all the necessary precautions to segregate the gluten-containing products from our nongluten containing products, we cannot absolutely make this guarantee; and, therefore, we do not recommend any of our products for those suffering from an intolerance to gluten. We are labelling those Quorn products, which do not contain added gluten to reflect this change.*

*Also, for your information, Quorn mince contains gluten from barley. We have no analysis, but our mince contains approximately 0.07% gluten, assuming that all of the protein in the malt extract is gluten.*

## Amy's Kitchen: Manhattan Veggie Burger

# Gluten-Free, High-Protein, Vegetarian Cookbook

This burger doesn't pack a high protein punch, but it is gluten free and can give you the hearty taste of a burger, if that's what you're craving. One serving gives you 3.8 grams of protein.

## Lightlife Vegetarian Products:

I just received this update about Lightlife, right from the company:

*We are happy to tell you that our Smart Dogs, Tofu Pups, Smart Strips Chick'N, Original Soy Tempeh, Three Grain Tempeh, Garden Vegetable Tempeh, Flax Tempeh and Wild Rice Tempeh are all gluten free!*

*Our manufacturing equipment is shared across products, however, we do a full and thorough facility cleaning before beginning the manufacturing process on a different product. In addition, all of the products are sorted and stored to avoid cross-contamination. We hope that this information is helpful and that you now feel comfortable trying all Lightlife Products without concern.*

*We appreciate your continued support as we strive to carry on the veggie revolution!*

## Gluten-Free Tofu

Yes, some tofu is considered gluten free. Below this heading, I have provided a list of the brand names that consider themselves uncontaminated with wheat products.

Tofu contains high levels of protective plant-based chemicals known to be highly helpful in preventing cancer. It specifically prevents breast and endometrial cancer in women and prostate cancer in men. However, as proven recently, too much of a good thing can cause problems as well as be a benefit. Just as an excess of natural estrogen may fuel the growth of a breast tumor, too much of the soy isoflavone *genistein* in concentrated form in many over-the-counter nutritional supplements, may set the stage for tumor development. But what about Asians who grow up on tofu? In Japanese women, who would consume the most soy-based products, since their youth, have the lowest rate of breast cancer in the world. So, don't stop eating tofu, just don't eat it every day.

One day, I tasted Italian-baked tofu and thought I was eating my dad's broiled chicken. Honestly, when I first tried tofu, I did not like it, because of its gelatinous texture. It had little taste, and I maintain that to this day. However, its texture can be changed by baking and frying it, which removes most of its water and leaves it tougher and chewier.

Tofu is a flavor chameleon, taking on the spices and herbs of whatever it is mixed with. I bet, if you tried each of the different textures of tofu, you would not even know some were tofu. For example, when I serve gluten-free lasagna, I mix ricotta and Romano cheeses with soft tofu. By doing this, I add a major source of protein to a pasta dish. No one has ever asked, "What is that unfamiliar taste?"

Five ounces of tofu gives you twenty-one grams of protein. This varies according to which tofu you choose. This means that you get three servings per sixteen-ounce container. Below is the list of gluten-free tofu manufacturers:

*Azumaya Tofu:* This tofu brand, made by Vitasoy USA Inc., is available in Extra Firm, Lite Extra Firm, Firm and Silken.

*House Foods:* makes a variety of different premium and organic tofus, both plain and seasoned. There customer service reps say, though, "If you are extra-sensitive and react to under 5 ppm of gluten, we do not recommend consuming our tofu."

Made by *Mori-Nu*, Morinaga tofu is non-GMO and labeled as gluten free, and is available in firm, light, soft, and silken varieties.

*Nasoya* is made by Vitasoy USA Inc. It comes in extra firm, firm, lite firm, soft, cubed and sprouted (tofu made with sprouted soybeans). The tofu is listed as gluten free on the company's website and is made in the same gluten-free facility.

*Small Planet Organics Tofu*: This minor manufacturer produces only tofu at a dedicated gluten-free facility.

*Trader Joe's* includes its store-brand High Protein Organic Super-Firm Tofu on its list of products with no gluten ingredients.

# Basic Recipe: Baked Tofu

### Changing the Texture of Tofu

Simply cut firm or extra firm tofu into half-inch slices and marinate them in a half-cup of tamari or 1/4 cup of Bragg's liquid aminos for about an hour. In preparation for baking, coat the slices with a thick coating of Brewers or Nutritional yeast.

Place tofu on a cookie sheet sprayed with olive oil nonstick cooking spray. Bake at 350° for 30-45 minutes. If you want to make your slices thicker, bake at a lower temperature for a longer period of time. The longer you bake the tofu, the more it becomes like jerky. So, the first time you bake tofu, begin to test the tofu's texture at 30 minutes, at a minimum, and every five minutes, thereafter.

# Recipe: Fried Tofu

Most people drain the water from tofu by placing it in a colander or tofu strainer for an hour. Otherwise, you can put slices between two small saucers and press them together over the sink to drain out the water. I admit, most of the time, I use neither method, because I bake the water right out of it.

Depending on how conscious of fat content you are, you can add olive oil to a frying pan and preheat it on medium heat. Then, simply fry chunks of tofu until they become golden brown. If you want tofu to take on the texture of cooked chicken, cut tofu into long thin strips and fry it for approximately twenty minutes on medium low heat, browning it slowly.

At this point, you have not flavored the fried tofu nor the

baked tofu, so the taste remains rather bland. In subsequent chapters we will learn to use these different textures as protein in our meal recipes.

### Soft Tofu

Soft tofu is used mostly for desserts, however I find it is an excellent choice to make a mock egg salad. You can also cut soft tofu into small cubes for miso soup.

### Kale: The New Chicken

Almost all scientists agree that global warming is a result of cattle grazing and leaving impenetrable gases in the atmosphere, instead of pastures being rich with vibrant fresh vegetables for human consumption. The fact that kale not only has the calcium and fiber everyone needs daily, it also has 2 grams of protein in each serving.

### Broccoli: The New Beef

A 100-calorie portion of broccoli has 8.29 grams of protein and the exact same caloric portion of sirloin contains 11.03 grams of protein. Though the broccoli pales by comparison in protein, it is rich in so many other nutrients.

### Gluten-Free Pasta

A 2-ounce portion of rice pasta has 4 grams of protein. A 2-ounce portion of Barilla gluten-free pasta, made of a combination of corn and rice, a bit more *al dente*, has the same amount of protein, but contains a lot less caloric content.

### Gluten-Free Bread

Most good, gluten-free bread is made with a combination of chickpea flour, potato flour, and rice flour. This gives the bread a richer, heavier feeling, but provides a little less protein per slice than gluten breads. At last count, 2-3 grams of protein can be gained from each slice of gluten-free bread.

### Nuts and Nut Flour

When a person begins using almond and other nut flours, it is clear that this gluten-free cook has become an expert, because of the amount of protein he or she is able to add to the result.

### Nutritional Yeast

Deactivated yeast, sold commercially as a food product in the form of flakes or as a yellow powder, can be found in the bulk aisle of most natural food stores. With 50 grams of protein out of 100 grams of yeast, this vitamin enriched seasoning and food source supplies B-complex vitamins and is free of sugar, dairy, and gluten.

If you have never tasted nutritional yeast, it has a strong flavor that is nutty and cheesy and can be used as a great topping for popcorn to make an evening snack into a protein-enriched snack.

*Concerned about yeast in your body?* Nutritional and Brewers yeast will not grow in your body like the yeast in bread. It provides trace minerals and vitamins rarely found in other food and is rich in protein, having 7 grams per tablespoon of Brewers and 4 grams per tablespoon for nutritional yeast. The difference between the two: Brewers yeast is grown on beet molasses and nutritional yeast is grown on cane and beet molasses.

### Eggs

By definition, according to Wikipedia: "Vegetarianism is the practice of abstaining from the consumption of meat, red meat, poultry, seafood and the flesh of any animal. It also includes abstention from by-products of animal *slaughter*." Then, by definition of the word *vegetarian*, it would be okay for a vegetarian to eat unfertilized, cage-free eggs. I do eat them and feel fine about it. Eggs are a great source of protein, giving us 6 grams of protein per egg.

### Milk Products and Cheese

Again, I don't use a great deal of milk products because they can cause mucous and sinus problems. I use organic 2% milk, which gets rid of most of the contraindication about milk products. If you have problems with cow's milk, try other milk, such as coconut, almond, or rice milk. All are gluten free.

### Cauliflower: The New Fish

In one head of cauliflower, you can glean 11 grams of protein. I know that it may be impossible to eat an entire head of cauliflower, but we are simply adding up protein-enriched substances, now, to help you make gluten-free, high protein choices for your next meal.

### Does Fruit Contain Protein?

The answer is *yes*. Not a great deal of protein, but avocado, dried fruit, such as raisins and apricots and berries are great to add to our meals for protein.

### Beans and Legumes

What is the difference between a bean and a legume? According to DailyHealthLesson.com, a legume is simply a plant with a fruit that grows in the form of a pod, though not all plants with pods are legumes. Classic legumes include peas, beans, or peanuts. Typically, the pods are not eaten, but things like green beans are an exception.

A bean is just a seed of a certain variety of plant species, but these days we refer to the whole plant as beans. Classic beans include green beans, lima beans, soybeans, chickpeas, kidney beans, pinto beans, or black-eyed peas.

Beans are low in fat and have no cholesterol. They are also high in fiber and supply nutrients such as folate, iron, potassium, and magnesium. They are also a terrific source of protein outside of meat and dairy, making them a popular choice for vegetarians. A typical serving of beans or legumes will give you from 10-39 grams of protein in one cup of nature's super food.

## Chapter Two:
## Herbs, Spices, and Thickening Agents

Many chefs start most dishes with a sautéed mixture of chopped onion, minced or mashed garlic, and chopped celery. You can either use olive oil as the healthiest choice, or do what I do and get the best of both tastes and health by using olive oil plus one teaspoon of butter as well. This way, you can get a hint of delicious, but don't risk heart failure in the process. Of course, if you're a vegetarian who doesn't use milk products, you could use a butter substitute.

The other spices I keep handy are below:

**Rosemary Powder** - I use a coffee grinder and make a powder out of a couple of seasoning containers of dried rosemary.

**Parsley** - fresh is best, but I don't mind dried.

**Sweet Basil** - I use fresh sweet basil, except in the winter when I use harvested basil leaves that I have frozen in a sealed, plastic bag. This will do in a pinch when the fresh isn't so available.

**Cumin** - this spice gives an Indian or Mexican flavor to any food.

**Paprika** - has the kick of a pepper, but not the heat.

**Ground Melange of Peppercorn** - different varieties of peppercorns give robust flavor to almost any food.

**Ginger** - you can buy ginger in a powder, freshly ground, or as a root. Personally, I buy ginger by the root, peel it, food process it, and then put it in a small jar covered with olive oil to protect it from aging. It will last about two months before growing mold.

**Oregano** - I grow fresh oregano in my garden for sauces. But when I make a salad dressing, I prefer the dried. Both are delicious.

**Mustard** - I actually use dried mustard in cooking much more than the condiment and never use mustard seed. My favorite mustard as a condiment is Maille's A l'Ancienne old-style Dijon mustard. It is expensive, but the best I have ever tasted.

**Mint** - Mint is the easiest herb to grow. If you enjoy tabouli in the summer, make sure you grow a small cluster. In a couple of years, you'll have to pull it out of your shrubs. This herb loves to grow, and it sure is rich with taste.

**Dill** - I use dill for vegetable stews, salad dressings, and my vegetarian broth.

**Cilantro** - This herb is great in so many dishes. I like to buy a bunch every other week and keep it in a sealed plastic baggy in the refrigerator to add to many recipes, especially Mexican salsas.

**Celery** - Though most people would consider this a vegetable, I'm more inclined to put celery in both categories. Its slight bitterness is great for soups, stews, stir fry, and raw in salads.

**Salt** - This is arguably the most important seasoning of any cooking. Without it, most meals would be bland and unexciting. Not all salt is created equal. Many types of salt exist; among a few are Himalayan pink salt, Kosher salt, sea salt, Celtic salt, and table salt. Not only do each of these salts contain different minerals, because they are refined in different parts of the world, but they also have vastly different flavor. One of the newest health discoveries of late is adding many different kinds of salt from around the world to your daily cuisine. This wide-spreading trend among healthy eaters is causing the prices to drop considerably and the availability to increase as well.

**Montreal Steak Seasoning** - Lastly, my season all for every thing but the kitchen sink is McCormick™ Montreal Steak Seasoning. Most vegetarians stick their noses up at this idea. But, McCormick swears it doesn't use any additives. This combination of garlic, peppers, and "seasons, undisclosed" does it for me in a pinch. You'll find it in many of my recipes.

**Xantham Gum** - For a thickening agent I almost always recommend a xantham gum and water mixture. You can usually find xantham gum in the health food section of the grocery store. Bob's Red Mill makes this. Bob's Red Mill is in most stores now, even Big Lots.

**Arrowroot** - I also recommend arrowroot as an alternative to xantham gum. Both are healthy choices and noncaloric.

# Chapter Three:
# Other Food Enhancements

Preparing a meal is like painting on a canvas. Each ingredient you choose adds a special color and texture to your food. Below, I list a few extra enhancements to create the most bang for your buck:

### Bragg's Liquid Aminos or Tamari

Bragg's is your definite choice for a gluten-free soy sauce substitute—great soy flavor with no gluten. Tamari is also a suitable substitute for soy sauce. Tamari has a richer flavor.

### Habeñero Pepper Paste

Buy a couple dried habeñero peppers. Place them directly on the burner (gas or electric) on the lowest heat. Get them soft and a bit crispy, but not burnt. Before they cool, split them, take out the seeds and cut off the stem. Afterward, place the pieces in a food processor with a little purified water. The result is a robust pepper paste that has a meat-like flavor.

### Sun-Dried Tomato Paste

Boil a few sun-dried tomatoes until they plump up a bit, no more than 3-5 minutes. Let them cool. Afterward, food process the cooled tomatoes. This, also, forms a robust pesto-like sauce that can be used to enhance food. (Try combining the habeñero and sun-dried tomato paste. Add this to gluten-free pasta for a delicious side dish topped with Romano cheese.)

### Vinegar

Rice Vinegar - Hypothetically, another contributing factor about Asian women not getting breast cancer is because of the amount of vinegar they consume. Frequently seen in Asian cuisine, rice vinegar is in almost every sauce and soup.

Apple Cider Vinegar - I use this most often in salads, as it comprises one-third of an Italian vinaigrette. I create flavored vinegar—such as with basil, tarragon, and dill—using apple cider vinegar. Many health experts suggest unrefined apple cider vinegar as a daily prescription.

Wine Vinegar - This combination of white vinegar and wine is also part of my trifecta for a perfect salad dressing.

Balsamic Vinegar - The Mercedes of vinegar, made from cooked trebbiano grapes, slowly aged in a variety of wooden casks and usually imported from Italy, this combination of sweet, mellow and tart tastes enhances just about anything. It is great with roasted garlic and olive oil to marinate grilled vegetables and also excellent in a vinaigrette. I also use it for marinades and in sauces. Definitely keep a bottle on hand.

### Fruit for Flavor

Adding lemon and lime juice or the rind from a lemon or lime to a meal not only gives it a tart kick, but also a burst of sunlight and freshness.

### Spirits

Red and white wine and sake are also among the flavorful additions you can bring to your palate. If you have left-over wine, save it in your refrigerator in an air-tight container for use in cooking.

### Oils

Olive Oil - If I could only have one oil, it would be chorlesterol-free olive oil, primarily, for health reasons. Low in saturated fat, it certainly adds a rich, robust flavor to everything you cook. One draw back exists though: you cannot use olive oil to fry something sweet or something with subtle flavors. It will overtake the tastes. Otherwise, I use olive oil in salad dressing, sauces, and stir-fries. I have asked around the Oriental Chef circuit. Olive oil is preferred over sesame oil for stir-fry. Always buy extra virgin olive oil, as it is the first press of the olives and has the most flavor.

When I was a child, my dad would buy olive oil and mix it with corn oil to dim down the flavor. I can't imagine doing that now. I either want the robust taste, or I choose another oil with little, to no taste, such as vegetable oil.

### Nut or Seed Oils

Sesame, peanut, and sunflower oil tend to be a little higher in saturated fat and a lot greater in robust taste. For instance, if I want the taste of sesame in a dipping sauce, I may add both the seeds and a little of the oil, to pump up the flavor. Some say a potato fried in peanut or sesame oil makes for great French fries. If you are a fried food lover, give it a try. But, do not indulge too often for the sake of your heart.

### Nut Butters

Tahini is sesame butter made from crushed sesame seeds. I use tahini a great deal in cooking. You really cannot make Mediterranean food without it. I know it is high in saturated fat—3 grams per 2 teaspoons, but the positive side is it also has 6 grams of protein for 2 teaspoons and no cholesterol. This ingredient is a must for hummus, some salad dressings, and cold sesame noodles. Definitely get a jar of tahini, but make sure it is smooth and creamy. A jar that has been sitting for too long will have the paste on the bottom and the oil floating on top. Check the expiration date!

# Gluten-Free, High-Protein, Vegetarian Cookbook

Peanut and Almond Butter are great to eat right on gluten-free bread. But, you can also make some great sauces for vegetables with a combination of the nut butter and chopped nuts. Most frequently, you will see this in Asian food.

If you have a Champion juicer, you can make your own nut butter by placing the juice stopper beneath the blade and letting the nut butter run out of the spout where the unused vegetable shavings usually disengage.

I love to roast raw almonds with Kosher salt and a spray of Bragg's liquid aminos. Roast the almonds in the oven at 275° for 2 hours. Let cool. Then create the aroma of your life by placing these babies in your Champion juicer. You will want to lick the spatula.

# Chapter Four:
# Cooking with Inspiration

When you realize that each time you eat, you have an opportunity to impact your health, you may consider making better choices each time. To do this, we must reach into our food palate and take out the proper amount of:

protein

fat; and

carbohydrates.

For a normal meal for a thriving adult, we need from 18-21 grams of protein for each meal to get the propper amount of energy from our food. Good sources of fat, such as avocado, can be great brain food, as the right fat is necessary for your brain to function. (*Grain Brain*, Perlmutter.)

But, when it comes to carbohydrates we have the added responsibility to separate the good from the unhealthy. Vegetables and fruit are in the category of complex carbohydrates. Bread, pastry, potato, even pasta are mostly simple carbohydrates. However, when food is fresh, instead of processed, you can be assured it is essentially better for you. Yes, broccoli may be a better carb than potato. But potato or rice is better than bread, even if it is gluten free. Our bodies can sense natural food and process it more easily.

A healthy food practice is to shop in the perimeter or outside of the food aisles in a grocery store. Most of the processed food is in the internal aisles. The fresh food stays in refrigeration around the perimeter of the building. Stick with this idea, and you'll be on the road to healthier eating.

So, to start our course in healthy, gluten-free, vegetarian recipes, we are going to begin with a broth.

## Recipe: Basic Broth

Bring to a boil in a saucepan:

6 cups of water

1/4 grated medium-sized onion

1/2 teaspoon chopped of crushed garlic

1 tabelspoon finely chopped fresh rosemary

 or 1/2 teaspoon rosemary powder

1/4 teaspoon chopped ginger

2 tablespoons olive oil

1/4 teaspoon chili paste—if you like a hot kick

1 tablespoon of parsley or dill

Some kind of interesting salt to taste. Your choice.

Let simmer for 15 minutes. In case you're a novice, simmer means to put on a very low heat with a lid on it.

Serving suggestions: Any time you need a meat broth, substitute this recipe. You can make soup; you can use this broth to cook vegetables, instead of stir-frying them, to avoid large amounts of fat; or you can add yogurt and make a cream sauce for pasta.

TIP: KEEP SOME OF THIS FROZEN FOR QUICK USE.

## SALAD

Salads are a mainstay in my home. I eat one of many varieties of salad, every day. For those who need to know step by step what to do to make a fresh salad, read on.

Before adding dressing, a fresh salad can consist of many ingredients. Just yesterday, a friend who has an herb garden ate a salad at my house. She was surprised I put fresh herbs in my salad. I couldn't believe that she would not know how wonderful some fresh oregano, thyme, or basil would taste combined with red leaf lettuce, tomato, cucumber, celery and a red onion. Here are some other options:

For the main ingredient of a salad, there is usually, but not always, some kind of lettuce. For instance, tabouli salad has parsley and mint; bean salad has every thing but lettuce. Salads are mixtures of things, usually with a dressing to enhance the flavors. I love to mix textures and flavors in salads. I can make a green salad, add a fried new potato, garbanzo beans, sautéed portabello mushroom (another good source of protein), and then tweek the flavor with a few bitter greens: endive, escarole, or dandelion. You may only want to add a small amount of the bitter herbs, but the combination of all the textures and tastes with a good Italian vinaigrette can give your taste buds a delightful surprise.

TIP: USING A METAL KNIFE WILL CAUSE LETTUCE TO TURN BROWN. IF YOU ARE NOT GOING TO USE ALL YOUR LETTUCE IMMEDIATELY, LET IT SOAK IN COLD WATER, AND TEAR GENTLY WITH YOUR HANDS, BEFORE REPLACING IT IN THE REFRIGERATOR.

Drain the water from your greens with a salad spinner or simply spill them into a collander and don't bother. A little water isn't going to hurt the flavor.

Some other fun ingredients to add to salads to beef up the protein and flavors are:

Raw or parboiled—slightly boiled and then rinsed immediately with cold water—broccoli.

Raw or parboiled asparagus

Artichoke hearts

A boiled egg

Beans of any kind

Carrots

Hearts of palm

Sliced mandarine oranges

Scallions

Chives

Cubed or grated cheese

Green or black olives

Hot pickled okra or pepperoncini

Once you have decided on ingredients, you are ready to add a dressing. You could, of course, buy a salad dressing. My favorite bottled dressing is Annie's Shitake and Sesame vinaigrette. (In the American dishes section of this book, I include my own version of a Shitake Sesame Salad Dressing, if you're into making it fresh.) Still, using a simple vinaigrette is simple.

## Recipe: Vinaigrette

Mix in a salad dressing container the proper amount of oil to vinegar to water ratio according to the bottle size. If you buy a salad dressing bottle, most have the ratio lines printed right on the bottle.

For the vinegar section, add red wine vinegar, and four dashes of balsamic vinegar.

Add a couple of tablespoons of pure water to diffuse the pungent flavor of the vinegar.

Then fill the rest of the cruette with virgin olive oil, but leave some room for the seasonings.

Add to this:

2 teaspoons of garlic powder

2 teaspoons of onion powder

1 teaspoon of ground melange of pepper or black pepper

1 teaspoon of lemon pepper seasoning

1/2 teaspoon of dill

1 1/2 teaspoons of dried oregano

1/2 teaspoon of your favorite salt

(Optional: 1/2 teaspoon of dried mustard)

Shake vigorously and let stand for 14.3 minutes. (I'm just kidding.) Just let it marinate for a short time. You can use this same dressing for any kind of salad and then drink the remaining juice from your salad bowl. It's great for your health.

## What Kind of Pasta Should I Buy?

Since we are working with a gluten-free diet, make sure the pasta has a gluten-free symbol on it. Your choices are rice pasta, corn pasta, or a combination of both rice and corn. Even companies like Barilla are getting on board with cheaper versions of what used to cost double what you pay now. Actually, if you look hard enough, even cereal aisles in your grocery store are now carrying gluten-free products.

Gluten-free products was a five billion dollar industry in 2013 and, I believe, that as people realize the advantages of a gluten-free diet, the demand will rise. More companies will get on board, and the prices will go down. So, look for price reduction in the future, especially with the bread.

After you choose the version of pasta you want, you must consider the size and style of pasta for the meal you decide to make. Remember, as a simple rule, small pasta is used for soups or as an added ingredient in a vegetable or bean salad. Larger pasta shapes are used for a main course.

## Other Important Cooking Facts:

Using a Pressure Cooker:

For cooking dried beans, I recommend using a pressure cooker. These pots used to be very dangerous. The newest electric versions are extremely safe and easy to use: however they are pricey. Keep looking for one in your nearest close-out store. I saw ten electric pressure cookers in a stack of boxes at a local Nashville closeout store for $39.99 a piece, which is a far cry from the $199.99 I paid for mine. Of course, read the instruction manual, recognizing that you can cut your cooking time by two hours when you cook beans. If you are busy, this is worth the extra cost of the pot. A stainless steel pressure cooker lasts practically forever, so it is a long-term investment.

**Great Fact:** If you find that what you cook in the pressure cooker is sticking to the bottom, you can find a stainless steel bowl and place it over a cup of water at the bottom of the pot and put what you're cooking in the stainless bowl, instead of directly into the bottom of the pan. Now the pressure cooker acts as a double boiler, preventing any burning of beans at the bottom of the pan.

**Fact Two:** Parboiling or Blanching

Periodically, you may want to quickly cook a vegetable to seal in its flavor. You can use parboiled vegetables such as broccoli and asparagus for freezing. Parboiling works in cold pasta salads, as well, or in other cold dishes and salads requiring crunchy vegetables.

I am not fond of raw broccoli, but I do love it parboiled or blanched, cooking it just enough for my taste. I feel the same about mushrooms. I will take the parboiled ones rather than the raw ones every time.

**Fun Fact:** An example of a time saving and cost saving measure is that you may want to take vegetables that are about to go bad, and parboil or blanch them in boiling water for 3 minutes. You can then place them in a sealed container, and the vegetables will now be good for another 4-5 days.

**Fact Three:** Preparing Tomatoes for Sauce

In the summer, when the tomatoes start to ripen faster than you can eat them, this is a perfect time to make salsas and fresh tomato-basil sauce. The blanching technique is simple.

Core the tomatoes, by cutting out the center. Set them in the bottom of a pot that has a lid. Pour enough boiling water over the top of the tomatoes to cover them. Replace the lid for five minutes. Open the lid and immediately pour off the boiling water and replace with with ice water. Yes, actually use ice cubes.

You will immediately see the skins separating from the meat of the tomato. After a couple of minutes in the cold bath of water, take one tomato at a time and pop off the skins, putting the meat of the tomato in a separate bowl or pot. If you get to a tomato that isn't ripe enough for it to pop out of its skin, you can use a paring knife to pull the skins off. They should come off easily. Composte the skins and drain the excess water off of the tomatoes in the bowl containing the tomato meat.

You have a choice, at this point:

Squeeze the tomatoes with your hand, until you have a pulpy mixture of small chunks of tomatoes and sauce or put them in a blender or food processor, which will make a pink liquid. Either way, you have prepared your fresh, ripe tomatoes for salsa or sauce.

## Chapter Five: Breakfast

A high-protein, low carbohydrate breakfast is not generally the American or European way. For many years, I ate boxed cereal and wondered why I always felt weak with hunger two hours later. I had no energy to get me through until lunchtime. If you follow a high-protein diet with gluten-free substances, you have just a few options for breakfast. You will, however, have to put most of your old ways aside, including drinking too much coffee, as the acid from the coffee causes hunger—more than not eating.

## Recipe: Breakfast—Steel-Cut Oats

(Serves 1)

Place in a saucepan:

1 cup of water

1/3 cup steel-cut oats

1/2 sliced banana or apple (for sweetness)

dash of cinnamon

dash of salt

Bring to a boil and let simmer until the oats are tender, then let sit, covered for 5 minutes, after you take the pot off of the heat. Sometimes, I add a little coconut or almond milk to it to give it a bit more protein. This, combined with a handful of almonds, should be enough to get you through until lunch.

## Recipe: Breakfast—Scrambled Tofu or Egg Substitute

(Serves 1)

Soft tofu or unfertilized and cage-free eggs, as I mentioned before, are a great source of protein and, for me, eggs don't challenge my vegetarian principles of killing to eat.

Place in Skillet with 1 teaspoon of olive oil or butter

6 oz. of scrambled tofu (crumbled soft tofu)

or use 2 eggs cooked any way

1 piece of gluten-free toast

1 cup of coffee

a piece of fruit (orange or apple for weight loss)

## Recipe: Weight Loss: Berries and Yogurt

(Serves 1)

As I said before, not all fruit has protein, but blueberries and berries, in general, are amazing for health. If you combine plain, fat-free yogurt with this fruit, it makes for a light breakfast. Personally, I eat very little in the morning. I'm just not hungry. Knowing that my body will tell me when it needs food, I respect its process. Listening to your body is the first step to losing weight and reaping the rewards of a great new diet.

## Recipe: Breakfast—Gluten-Free Pancakes

(Serves 4)

Bob's Red Mill™ Products are great products for people who have gone completely gluten free.

Simply follow the directions on the bag.

The difference will be this: Instead of using maple syrup, try using Agave nectar, which is better for your glycemic index. In other words, since agave is a fruit sugar, it will process slower than syrup, causing you less of a spike in your glucose reading. This fact is great if you are a diabetic and splurging on one pancake every three months. If the plain agave nectar doesn't suit you, try it with a few drops of maple flavoring added.

Of course, I would be remiss if I didn't mention that you need protein with this meal, or you will definitely be gaining weight, so try adding some nuts to the top of the pancake or add an egg or two.

# Chapter Six:
# Snacks

Most healthy eating programs include smaller meals and a couple snacks during the day. For gluten-free, healthy snacks, here are a few suggestions:

**Protein Bars:**

Think Thin™, Bonk Breaker™, Quest Bar™, Pure Fit™, and Luna™ are my favorite protein bars. I like to keep a few of these bars in my home, when I am in a hurry and need a quick pick me up. Check out the different flavors and choose a bar that will satisfy your sweet tooth and your hunger. Also, remember, with a snack, you should try to gain about 10-14 grams of protein.

**Protein Drinks:**

ISoPure™, Garden of Life Raw Organic Meal™, Rainbow Light Protein Enegizer™, NutriBiotic Rice Protein™, Navitas Natural Organic Hemp Powder™, and Jarrow's Formula, Brown Rice Protein™ are the best out there for protein drinks.

# Gluten-Free, High-Protein, Vegetarian Cookbook

Most people mix these with almond, rice, or coconut milk. I still use regular 2% milk, and I'm apt to switch between organic cow's milk and coconut milk.

### Edamame

You may already be saying to yourself: "I thought all soy products have gluten!" You would be incorrect. The truth about soy is that most of the soy we buy is modified and texturized and fermented, which all cause soy products to contain some gluten. However, soybeans in the pod are not modified and have great nutritional value. One serving has 10 grams of protein.

Take a cup of frozen edamame (bought in the frozen vegetable section of your grocery) and put them in a sauce pan with water to cover the top.

Bring the water to a boil. After the water boils, time it for five minutes. Drain the water, add salt to taste, and pop the beans from the pod into your mouth. DON'T EAT THE POD!

I have replaced my salty evening snack with this tasty delight. I promise you, you won't be sorry, if you have never tried them at a Japanese restaurant.

### Lupini Beans

The Italians have an old time favorite that has a little bit more protein than edamame. Lupini is also a bean in a pod. These days you can buy them in the Italian section of any grocery chain.

Drain the jar of the salty brine. Add new, fresh water and place the jar back in the refrigerator. Change the water for two days in a row; otherwise, the beans retain too much salt.

After the two days, add a few tablespoons of the vinaigrette dressing in Chapter Four, shake it up good, and you have a snack that has 13 grams of protein for 1/2 cup.

### Yogurt

If you are not dairy free, plain yogurt is always good. I love organic plain yogurt, Greek Style. Some people like to add a bit of agave nectar. Not a problem. You also can add a bit of berries or some sliced banana for a great, healthy snack, and this is great for your digestive system. So, if you haven't eaten it for breakfast, you may consider it for a snack.

### Cottage Cheese

Low fat, organic cottage cheese is also great for a snack if you are not lactose intolerant.

### Gluten-Free Crackers and...

As the years go by, more and more gluten-free products appear on the grocery shelf. Four really good crackers exist now, in my estimation. The best is Nut Thins™ for sure, especially since nuts give you protein with your snack. These crackers come in different flavors. But, if you plan to have your crackers with hummus or cheese, I'd recommend getting the crackers with a hint of sea salt.

## Recipe: Snack—Hummus

Chickpeas are a wonderful source of protein—7 grams for 1/2 cup. Hummus, made of garbanzo beans or chickpeas, is especially good with gluten-free crackers.

Combine in a food processor or blender:

One 15-16 ounce can of chick peas, drained of water

1/2 teaspoon of chopped garlic or 1 clove

3 tablespoons of fresh lemon juice

2 tablespoons tahini

1/4 teaspoon salt

1 teaspoon of olive oil

This is the basic recipe. Food process until beans are completely crushed. If you choose to use a blender, you can add about 1/4-1/2 cup of warm water or the juice from the can, so that you get more of a liquid version of hummus; otherwise, your blender won't mix the beans. I actually prefer the hummus to be more liquid than solid.

Garnish with fresh parsley sprigs. Make a small well in the

center of the hummus and drizzle with olive oil. Then, sprinkle with paprika.

### Variations of Hummus

If you want to try a few different varieties of this recipe, try adding any of the following:

1/4 teaspoon onion salt, or

1/4 teaspoon curry seasoning, or

1/4 cup sun-dried tomato paste from Chapter Three, or

1/4 cup habeñero paste from Chapter Three, or

1/4 cup of sweet basil pesto from the Italian Recipes.

# Chapter Seven: Dinner and Lunch Recipes

These recipes are divided into ethnicity. At the beginning of each section, you will find individual recipes, each containing a short explanation of its origin and some basic tips on preparation.

### Size Matters

The size and shape of vegetables vary, so exact measurements do not really exist. Here are a few helpful hints to keep you on track with not-so-precise measurements:

Onion size: A large-sized onion is about the shape of a tennis ball. If you use a huge onion and the recipe calls for a 1/4 of an onion, use less.

Scant: Use a litle less than the amount indicated

Herb and spice amount: Start with the amount indicated and add more to your individual taste. The amounts shown are a starting point. Everyone has his or her own taste buds.

## Gluten-Free, High-Protein, Vegetarian Cookbook

You will know how much salt and spice and herbs to add, once you taste your food. Always remember to start with a smaller amount. *You can always add, but you can't subtract spice.*

# NORTH AMERICAN DISHES

## Recipe: Complete Meal—Tiger Food

Gluten-Free Tofu with Mixed Vegetables

(Serves 2)

Here's a fast way to get a great mixture of fresh veggies and protein. I serve Tiger Food most often at lunch or even at a brunch, because the texture of the food looks little like scrambled egg. High in protein because of the tofu, and full of wonderful vitamins because of the fresh vegetables, this meal will provide you with plenty of energy.

Sauté in 2 teaspoons of olive oil:

1 teaspoon of chopped garlic

1/4 cup of chopped onion

1/2 cup of mushrooms

1/3 cup of chopped red or green bell pepper or both

When mixture begins to brown, add:

1 diced tomato

8 ounces of crumbled firm or extra-firm tofu

1 dash of rubbed thyme

1 teaspoon of basil

4 sprigs of fresh, chopped parsley or cilantro

2 tablespoons of fresh chives or scallions

Cover and let steam for two minutes on low heat. Top with cheddar or mozzarella cheese, if you are not worried about extra fat and are not lactose intolerant. To add a little safe carbohydrate with this meal, you can serve with brown or jasmine rice.

# Recipe: Lunch Meal—Barbecued Vegetable Roll-Ups

(Serves 2)

This recipe requires barbecue sauce, so that means you either already have a favorite, or you must look for one that is gluten free. Most healthfood stores or grocery stores with a health-food section will have a barbecue sauce that you will enjoy.

In a frying pan, sauté:

1/4 cup of chopped onion

1/4 teaspoon of chopped garlic

1/4 cup of chopped pepper—any kind

2 cups of finely chopped vegetables (you can use chopped zucchini, squash, cabbage, or broccoli.)

Let simmer on low with 1/2 cup barbecue sauce.

Preheat another large skillet (I use a cast iron skillet to soften corn tortillas). Place one large burrito-sized, gluten-free corn tortilla in the skillet. Let it soften and brown slightly with no oil on both sides. If you want some added flavor, after you turn it, melt some mozzarella, goat, or cheddar cheese on top of the tortilla.

If you want to add the flavor of cheese, but don't eat milk products, try sprinkling some nutritional yeast on the tortilla.

Place half of the barbecue mixture on the tortilla. Slide it on to a plate and roll it up.

For a different flavor, you can put some brown mustard on the top of the roll-up.

# Recipe: Dinner Meal—Chicken-Style Stroganoff

(Serves 5)

This recipe will stir your desire for richer vegetarian food with taste and texture. I developed this recipe after trying Smart Strips Chick'n™ from *Lightlife*™. This protein texture is great in sauces and stews, as well as in this hearty dish.

In a deep skillet combine:

1 cup of Chick'n Smart Strips

1/2 cup of red wine

2 cups of water

1 teaspoon of chopped garlic

3/4 cup of coconut milk

3/8 cup of tamari

1/2 cup of sliced mushrooms

2 teaspoons of tomato paste (You can use the sundried paste.)

1 medium-sized, chopped onion

1/2 teaspoon of McCormick™ Montreal Steak Seasoning

1/2 teaspoon of rosemary powder or 1 teaspoon of fresh rosemary

1/2 teaspoon of dried mustard

Let simmer for 10 minutes, or until the strips and onions are tender. Just after you remove from heat, to thicken, add either a mixture of 1 teaspoon xanthan gum and 1/2 cup water, or if you don't mind using milk products, add 1/2 cup Then, let this sit while you boil your pasta.sour cream.

For the xanthan mixture, usually, I use a small jar to mix it with a few quick shakes. (Most bottled salad dressing use xantham gum as a thickening agent. It is also used in most gluten-free breads.) Xanthan is, basically, noncaloric and binds with water causing an egg-like mixture. So, even one teaspoon with a 1/2 cup of water will give you a thick and rich mixture for your gravies and dressings.

Use, of course, gluten-free noodles. With this kind of meal, Thai rice noodles used for Pad Thai are the perfect substitute for fettuccini or egg noodles. Follow the instructions on the package to soften the noodles. Then, serve with the chicken mixture.

A nice, huge dish of sautéed kale or broccoli goes well with this meal.

Gluten-Free, High-Protein, Vegetarian Cookbook

# Recipe: Quick Meal—Veggie Burgers, Sweet Potato Fries, and Salad.

(Serves 1 or more)

For someone on the go, this is a fast way to get the meal on the table and eat healthy food.

You only have two items to prepare: the sweet potato fries and the salad. You can wash and slice a sweet potato in a few minutes. Fry the slices slowly on medium low until golden brown and tender using 1 tablespoon of olive oil.

While the potato is frying, create a salad. You can use whatever greens and veggies you have handy. I like to keep some prewashed organic greens in the refrigerator. Start with some greens. Add a bit of onion, some celery, a cut tomato, and some sliced cucumbers. Use the vinaigrette recipe from Chapter Three to dress the salad or use a gluten-free bottled dressing.

When everything is five minutes from being on the table, put your Amy's Kitchen™ veggie burgers in the frying pan or on a George Forman Grill™ and fry until they are golden brown.

Since you're eating a potato with this meal, I'd go without any bread. Serve the burger hot with the fries and a side of salad, or place everything on the plate at once. I love when a good vinaigrette gets mixed into the rest of the meal.

# Recipe: Meal—Kale Stew with Quorn Nuggets

(Serves 4)

In the winter months, I crave a hearty stew like this recipe, made with Quorn Chicken-Style Nuggets. You may substitute some of the vegetables with your favorites, but the kale gives the stew a robust flavor.

In a large pot or pressure cooker combine:
2 cups of water
1 cup of diced tomatoes with the juice, when in season
(if not in season, use a 16-ounce can of diced tomatoes)
1 1/2 cups of Quorn Chicken-Style Nuggets
2-3 cups of kale
1 diced potato
2 sliced carrots
1 large onion, diced in large chunks
1/2 cup of diced celery
1 cup of baby lima beans
1/2 cup of purple hull peas

Season with:
2 teaspoons of Montreal Steak Seasoning
1 tablespoon of olive oil
(Optional: 1 tablespoon of butter)
1 teaspoon of rosemary powder
1 teaspoon of dried or fresh dill
Salt to taste.

Let this simmer slowly, if you're cooking on the stove top,

## Gluten-Free, High-Protein, Vegetarian Cookbook

until all the vegetables and beans are tender.

Even if you're just cooking for yourself, you can keep this in your refrigerator or freezer and have it as leftovers all week. Remember, vegetarian protein does not go bad as quickly as meat does.

If you use a pressure cooker, this may take about 8 minutes on high. Decompress the pressure cooker and taste the beans and kale. When they are tender, the stew is done.

# Recipe: Main Course Protein— Barbecued Tempeh

(Serves 2)

I love barbecue sauce, as you may have noticed already. I realized—after I became a vegetarian—that I was not craving the ribs or pulled pork, but the tangy sauce, instead. This recipe is so simple and gives you the feeling of a picnic.

In a frying pan sauté:
1/4 cup of chopped onion
1/4 teaspoon of chopped garlic
1/4 cup of chopped pepper—any variety
8 ounces of tempeh, crumbles or sliced
(Lightlife™, any version)

Fry mixture until tempeh becomes a little crispy and onions are translucent. Add 1/2 cup of your favorite gluten-free barbecue sauce and let simmer on low for 2-4 minutes. Serve this hot on a gluten-free bun or over brown jasmine rice.

Gluten-Free, High-Protein, Vegetarian Cookbook

# Recipe: Side Dish—Stuffed Yellow Squash

(Serves 4)

This recipe takes the bland flavor of yellow squash to an all-time high. I have grown sage ever since I started my herb garden, but hardly ever use it. This recipe and the following recipe for stuffed zucchini combines the powerful taste of sage with the subtle taste of baby yellow squash and zucchini. In fact, you can cook both zuchini and squash side by side and serve them as a side dish with a protein entrée.

Slice in half, from top to bottom:

2 young yellow squash—no bigger than 6 or 7 inches long. If you let yellow squash get bigger than this, it becomes bitter. Dig out the softer, seeded center with a teaspoon, leaving only a 1/4" of squash as a holder for the stuffing.

In a sauté or frying pan:

Melt 2 tablespoons of butter (or use 2 tablespoons of olive oil)

Add:

5 finely chopped sage leaves

1/4 cup chopped celery (use the leaves too)

1/4 cup finely chopped onion

salt and ground pepper to taste

When mixture heats and begins to fry, turn off the heat. Add 1/4 cup of gluten-free bread crumbs to the mixture.

HINT: WHEN A LOAF OF GLUTEN-FREE BREAD GETS HARD OR STALE, LEAVE THE REST OF IT OUT OF THE BAG TO DRY COMPLETELY. THEN MIX IT IN A FOOD PROCESOR TO BECOME CRUMBS.

Stuff the squash with the sauté mixture.

Cover and bake at 350° in a baking dish with 1/4 inch of water at the bottom of the pan for 1/2 hour or until tender. Just before serving, uncover the top and let the squash brown for 5 minutes.

(Optional: Add 1/4 cup finely chopped Granny Smith apple to the sauté with a dash of nutmeg, for a slightly different taste.)

# Recipe: Side Dish—Stuffed Zucchini Squash with Protein

(Serves 4)

This recipe for stuffed zucchini combines the powerful taste of sage with the subtle taste of zucchini.

Slice in half, from top to bottom one large zucchini:

Dig out the softer, seeded center with a teaspoon, leaving only a 1/4" of squash as a holder for our stuffing.

In a sauté or frying pan:

Melt 3 tablespoons of butter (or use 3 tablespoons of olive oil)

Add:

1 cup of gluten-free, crumbled, brown rice tempeh

5 finely chopped sage leaves

1/4 cup chopped celery (use the leaves too)

1/4 cup finely chopped onion

1/4 cup chopped mushrooms

1 teaspoon dried or a couple sprigs of fresh parsley

2 dashes of cayenne pepper

2 dashes of paprika

Salt and ground pepper to taste

When this mixture heats and begins to fry, turn off the heat. Add 1/2 cup of gluten-free bread crumbs to the mixture. The desired texture is like bread stuffing.

Stuff the squash with the mixture.

Cover and bake at 350° in a baking dish with 1/4 inch of

water at the bottom of the dish for 45 minutes or until tender. Just before serving, uncover the top and let the zucchini brown for 5 minutes.

# Gluten-Free, High-Protein, Vegetarian Cookbook

## Recipe: Meal—Tofu, Herb Vegetable Soup

(Serves 4)

This recipe can be used with or without egg white. If you prefer the texture, but don't want the egg, you can use 1/2 cup of water and one teaspoon of xantham gum and mix with a beater until it looks like raw egg white. Then just mix into the soup.

Preparing the herb broth:
Bring to a boil:
4-6 cups of water
1/4 grated medium-sized onion
1/2 teaspoon of chopped or crushed garlic
1 tablespoon of fresh or dried chopped rosemary
1/4 teaspoon of ginger
2 tablespoons of olive oil
1/4 teaspoon of chili paste—increase if you like heat
1 tablespoon chopped parsley
Salt to taste.

When the water boils, add 1/2 a cup of small-sized, gluten-free soup noodles. Many brands of gluten-free pasta exist now. Just find a shape that is small, so you don't over do it with the carbohydrates. Let the noodles cook for about 10 minutes, stirring occasionally.

Add chopped vegetables:
Small amounts of some or any of the following:
Broccoli, celery, carrots, spinach, bok choy, or Chinese nappa.
Add 1/3 block of cubed, firm, gluten-free tofu from the list

in Chapter One. Boil for another 3-4 minutes.

In a separate bowl combine:

1/4 cup egg substitute or 1/4 cup egg whites

Whisk in 2 tablespoons of Romano cheese, if you are not lactose intolerant. Pour this mixture into the boiling soup, while stirring with a whisk. After one minute, take the sauce pot off of the burner.

Let stand uncovered for 2 minutes. Top with chopped scallions or chives.

(Optional: You may substitute one whole stalk of lemon grass for the rosemary, but you must heat the broth and let it simmer for 15-20 minutes to extract the flavor from the lemon grass, first, then continue with the recipe, disposing of the lemon grass stalk, before eating the soup.)

Gluten-Free, High-Protein, Vegetarian Cookbook

# Recipe: Main Course Protein— Tofu Burgers

(Serves 4)

This is a great, high-protein, low-fat recipe for someone on the go. You can make an entire batch and keep the burgers in the refrigerator for a week or even freeze the patties to be fried or reheated at a later time. You can, also, use these as a replacement for meatballs, when preparing spaghetti sauce.

Mix the following in a food processor on pulse setting until you have a blended mixture of small pieces, don't liquify it:

1 cup gluten-free of bread crumbs or 1 cup of cooked white rice

1/4 cup of nutritional yeast

1/2 cup of grated Romano cheese

1 tablespoon of fresh or dried dill

1 teaspoon of dried basil or five chopped fresh basil leaves

1 teaspoon of garlic powder (not salt)

1 teaspoon of onion powder (not salt)

1 teaspoon of mustard powder

1 teaspoon of Montreal Steak Seasoning

1 teaspoon of dried parsley or a couple of sprigs of freshly chopped parsley

1/2 teaspoon of ground melange of peppers

1/2 teaspoon of salt

1/2 teaspoon of celery seed

2 eggs or substitute 1/2 cup of xantham gum and water mixture, whisked or shaken in a jar

2 chopped scallions

1/4 cup of chopped pepper (hot, if you like)

1 tablespoon of tahini

2 tablespoons of ketchup or tomato paste

1 tablespoon of tamari or Bragg's liquid aminos

Add to the vegetable mixture, after you have drained the excess water, three-quarters of a 16-ounce container of firm tofu, in a food processor. (This is one of those times you need to drain the water from the tofu.) Mix all ingredients, using the pulse setting, again, just until the tofu separates and mixes with the vegetables. Take the mixture out of the food processor and place in a mixing bowl.

Mix in the last quarter of the tofu into the raw tofu mixture with your hands. I have also used my mix master with the bread dough paddle to do this to keep my hands cleaner. Either way is fine. You may need to add a bit more gluten-free bread crumbs to get a moist, but not wet, mixture in either case.

Preheat a skillet with a dash of olive oil or cooking spray and fry patties until golden brown. Remember, the thicker you make the patties, the slower you should cook them. If you want to make vegetarian meatballs for sauce, never add them to the sauce while cooking. They will immediately break apart in your sauce and cause a mess. Place the fried vegetarian meatballs on a plate and serve a dipper of sauce and cheese (or substitute nutritional yeast) on top.

## Recipe: Side Dish—Skillet Fried Potatoes with Rosemary

(Serves 3)

I was brought up on fried potatoes. We had them at least once a week. Of course, in the early 1960s, we never thought of making potatoes interesting. They were simply a cheap staple—a way to fill our bellies. These days, I look for low fat, tasty ways to make potatoes into mouth-watering side dishes.

In a large skillet combine:

1 tablespoon each of corn oil, olive oil, and peanut oil

Add 4 thinly sliced and peeled new potatoes

Let the potatoes fry for fifteen minutes on medium heat.

Add:

1 sliced onion

1/2 teaspoon of garlic powder

1/2 teaspoon of rosemary powder or 1 teaspoon of rosemary

1/2 teaspoon of ground pepper melange

1 teaspoon of dried parsley

Salt to taste

Cover skillet until potatoes and onions are tender. Then, remove lid and let the potatoes get brown and crispy.

# Recipe: Side Dish—Shitake Sesame

(Serves 8)

I rarely use any other salad dressing besides the vinaigrette and this shitake sesame.

Soak 5 medium-sized, dried, shitake mushrooms in 1 1/2 cups of boiling water for one hour with a lid.

Remove the mushrooms and save the water.

Toast 6 tablespoons of sesame seeds. (In a cast iron skillet, without oil, sprinkle seeds evenly at the bottom. Place skillet on medium low heat. Shake the skillet every couple of minutes until the first seed pops. Then the sesame seeds are toasted.)

Place all of these ingredients in a blender:

5 hydrated shitake mushrooms

6 tablespoons of toasted sesame seeds

10 tablespoons of tamari

1/2 teaspoon of xantham gum

1 1/2 cups of shitake mushroom water

1/4 cup of grape seed or olive oil

1/4 cup of sesame seed oil

3/4 cup of corn oil

1/2 cup of unrefined apple cider vinegar

1/4 cup of red wine vinegar

Blend until smooth. Keep refrigerated to store.

# Recipe: Main Course— Basic Bean Recipe

(Serves 8-10)

This recipe was Hilda's, an elderly Spanish woman I met in New York in 1980. She made the best beans and rice. Over the years, the recipe has been transformed to more of an American and Cuban style. The original recipe required a Mexican Adobe spice, which contained MSG. Well, *we ain't having none of that nasty chemical!* Also, the original recipe had calabaza, which is a Mexican sweet pumpkin that is often hard to acquire. So, I added carrot, instead.

Place in a large sauce pan:

1 pound of beans (pinto, white, or northern)

2 quarts of water

Bring the water to a boil for ten minutes. Take the pot off of the heat and let it stand overnight or for four hours, minimum. Pour off the water to remove the chemical that causes gastro intestinal problems.

Add 2 quarts of fresh spring or purified water to the beans.

Mix in:

1/2 teaspoon cumin

1 large or 2 small whole onions (grated or chopped)

1/4 cup of olive oil

1 heaping teaspoon of chopped garlic or three whole cloves

2 stalks of chopped, grated or food-processed celery

2 chopped, grated, or sliced carrots

6 bay leaves

1 teaspoon of salt

1 tablespoon of tamari or Bragg's liquid aminos

1 tablespoon of agave nectar

1/4 cup tomato paste or one cup of chopped fresh tomato

2 tablespoons of vinegar (I prefer Balsamic)

1/4 cup of chopped cilantro leaves

If you are using a conventional stove, bring the water to a boil, then reduce heat to a simmer. Beans may take up to 2 1/2 hours to become tender. You could also cook the beans for 8 hours in a crockpot.

(Optional: If you are using a pressure cooker, reduce the water to 5 cups and the time to 30-35 minutes.)

(Optional: Before serving, top with one or more of the following: salsa, plain yogurt, sour cream, chopped onion, grated cheddar cheese, or black olives.)

Gluten-Free, High-Protein, Vegetarian Cookbook

# Recipe: Main Course—Cuban Black Beans

(Serves 8-10)

I have tasted many black bean recipes from hearty to bland. This one is my own and is spicy and hearty. You can eat these beans as soup topped with a dollop of sour cream, yogurt, or grated cheddar cheese. In Cuba, they serve the beans with spicy sour greens and rice.

Place in a sauce pan:

1 pound of black beans

2 quarts of water

Bring the water to a boil for ten minutes. Take the pot off of the heat and let it stand overnight for four hours, minimum. Pour off the water to remove the chemical that causes gastro intestinal problems.

Add 2 quarts of fresh spring or purified water to the beans.

Mix in:

1/2 teaspoon cumin

1 large or 2 small whole onions (grated or chopped)

1/2 cup of chopped sweet banana peppers

1/4 cup of olive oil

2 heaping teaspoon of chopped garlic or three whole cloves

2 stalks of chopped, grated or food-processed celery

1 chopped, grated, or sliced carrots

6 bay leaves

1 teaspoon of salt

2 tablespoon of nutritional yeast

5 dashes of Tobasco™ Sauce

2 juiced limes or 1/8 cup of apple cider vinegar

1/4 cup of tamari or Bragg's liquid aminos

1 tablespoon of paprika

1/2 cup chopped cilantro leaves

If you are using a conventional stove, bring the water to a boil, then reduce heat to a simmer. Beans may take up to 2 1/2 hours to become tender. You could also cook the beans for 8 hours in a crockpot.

(Optional: If you are using a pressure cooker, reduce the water to 5 cups and the time to 30-35 minutes.)

(Optional: Before serving, top with one or more of the following: salsa, plain yogurt, sour cream, chopped onion, grated cheddar cheese, or black olives.)

# Recipe: Condiment—Fresh Salsa

(Serves 4)

The taste of this salsa goes with anything from gluten-free corn chips to scrambled eggs. It is very authentic and tastes better than any I've ever had.

Begin with either:

1 cup of chopped very ripe tomatoes, or

1 16 oz. can of diced tomatoes

Add very finely chopped:

1/8 cup of onion

1/8 cup of pepper—sweet bananas work great

Note: I always start with peppers that are not hot and add cayenne pepper to increase the heat.

Add:

1 tablespoon of chopped chili peppers

1/2 teaspoon of crushed garlic

2 dashes of Tobasco™ sauce

The juice of one lime

1/4 cup of chopped fresh cilantro leaves

1/2 teaspoon of sugar or 1 teaspoon agave nectar

Salt to taste

Cayenne pepper to make extra hot

One dash of cumin to taste.

# Recipe: Meal—Salad with Chik'n or Baked Tofu

(Serves 1 or more)

Quick and tasty meals are my motto. This meal can be prepared in ten minutes, and it provides you with fresh, uncooked vegetables and protein for energy. You can use any dressing that is gluten free or use the vinaigrette or shitake dressing from this book.

Prepare the Lightlife Chik'n Strips™ by frying or baking. If you want to use tofu, use either the baked version or the Italian strips from the Italian section in this book.

Chop into a large salad bowl:

Any lettuce, but iceberg

Celery

Onion

Cucumber

Tomato

Fresh herbs, such as basil, oregano, thyme, chives or parsley

(Make as much salad as you or your family can eat.)

Chop up the baked or fried Chik'n strips or tofu on top of the lettuce and serve with a salad dressing of your choice.

Extra toppings: Boiled egg, black olives, cheese, French fried potatoes, or all of the above.

# Recipe: Meal—Yeast Gulch Gravy & Buddha Bowl

(Serves 2)

You can use this gluten-free gravy from this recipe to replace any hearty-tasting meat gravy for mashed potatoes, rice, or a meatfree loaf.

To create the Buddha Bowl, simply place 1 cup of steamed kale at the bottom of a large bowl. On top, place 1/2 cup of brown rice, a 1/2 cup of Cuban black beans to cover. Then top with crispy baked tofu. Then smother with this protein-enriched yeast gravy.

This is a hearty meal for a person who has been working out in the yard all day. If you've been behind the computer, you might want to just eat half of this portion.

Recipe for the gravy only:

Mix ingredients in blender:

1 cup of water

1/2 tablespoon of onion powder

1/4 cup of tamari

1/2 cup of nutritional or Brewer's yeast

1/2 tablespoon of xantham gum

2 dashes of rosemary powder

2-3 dashes of white pepper

For an extra zest: Add one teaspoon of the habañero paste and one teaspoon of the sun-dried tomato paste from Chapter 3.

Let simmer on low in a sauce pan until warm.

# Recipe: Side Dish—Rosemary Mashed Potatoes

(Serves 4)

No matter where I get invited to dinner, if the friend or relative is serving mashed potatoes, he or she puts me in charge. This mashed potato recipe will replace your old one, I promise.

Boil 6 medium potatoes cut into cubes. I like to use new potatoes so peeling them isn't required. But, I would suggest peeling a dirtier, brown potato.

After boiling for approximately 15 minutes, when the potatoes are tender (when you are easily able to cut a potato piece with a fork), then drain off the hot water in a colander.

At the bottom of your Mixmaster bowl, place 1/4 of a stick of butter. Place the hot potatoes on top of the butter to melt it.

Add 1/2 cup of plain, organic yogurt

Salt to taste

1/2 teaspoon of white ground pepper

1 teaspoon of ground rosemary (If you haven't read the section on spices, I grind my rosemary with a coffee grinder to make a powder.)

Mix slowly, first, then turn up the Mixmaster to medium high and whip the potatoes before serving.

Gluten-Free, High-Protein, Vegetarian Cookbook

# Recipe: Side Dish—Marinated Roasted Vegetables

(Serves 1 or more)

Sometimes we crave the flavor of something grilled. This recipe is simple. It does require, however, a nonstick vegetable grill basket. Of course, you could, also, use your oven and broil the vegetables from the top.

Prepare this dressing first:
Slowly roast a bulb of garlic for one hour in your oven or toaster oven at 275°. When it cools, cut off the top of the garlic bulb with a sharp knife. The cloves should pop out when you squeeze the bulb.

Place the cloves in a blender with:
1/4 cup of olive oil
1/8 cup of Balsamic vinegar
Coarsely ground melange of peppers and salt to taste.
Blend to make a creamy dressing.

Preparing the vegetables:
Choose vegetables such as eggplant, zucchini, squash, asparagus, broccoli, cauliflower, onion, tomatoes, and peppers.

Cut slices of each vegetable 1/2" thick. Toss vegetables in the dressing mixture. I like to toss them in a large, plastic enclosed container. Dump in the veggies, pour in the dressing, put on the lid, and shake!

Grill or broil for about 15 minutes or until the vegetables are the desired texture for you.

Hint: If you don't have time to make a dressing, use a gluten-free Italian-style dressing.

## Recipe: 10-Minutes Meal— Vegetarian Reuben Sandwich

(Serves 2)

Yes, we can still eat the occasional sandwich and still be gluten free. But, because most of the world hasn't caught on, we probably will have to make it ourselves.

Prepare 1000 Island Dressing first:
Mix together in a bowl:
2 tablespoons of cold-pressed, grape seed, vegan mayonaise
1/2 teaspoon of sweet pickle relish
1/2 teaspoon of gluten-free barbecue sauce
1/2 teaspoon of gluten-free ketchup
1 dash of rubbed thyme

Sauté in one teaspoon of olive oil:
1 tablespoon of chopped onion
1/4 teaspoon of chopped garlic
1 tablespoon of chopped green or red pepper, or both

Add one package of sliced, gluten-free tempeh. Brown on both side to gather the flavor of the onion and garlic frying with it.

(Optional: Melt grated cheddar or mozzarella cheese on top. Cover and let stand off of the heat.)

Heat 1/2 cup of drained, fresh sauerkraut.

On toasted, gluten-free bread, apply 1000 Island dressing on one side and old-style Dijon mustard on the other. Put 1/2 of sauté mixture on two sandwiches. Top with warm sauerkraut. Add sliced tomatoes and serve.

## Recipe: Side Dish—Tofu Au Gratin
(Serves 4)

Though this recipe does not use cheese, the consistency reminds me of au gratin. You will not believe how simple this protein-fortified recipe is to create. If you are fond of Indian curries, this bold side dish will go well with a fresh vegetable or salad. Consider lentil soup and a few gluten-free crackers.

Slice into long, thin strips:
10 ounces of firm tofu
Place into a casserole dish.

Mix in a small bowl:
4 tablespoons of vegan mayonaise
1 teaspoon of curry powder

Pour the mayonaise mixture on top of the tofu.
Bake uncovered for 10-15 minutes at 350°

# JAPANESE DISHES

## Recipe: Dressing—Miso-Carrot

(Serves 4)

Many miso pastes are made with gluten. So, the first thing you must do is a little research, when you buy your miso. Miso frequently, though not always, contains grain. Check the label for gluten-containing grains like barley (*mugiortsubu* in Japanese), wheat (*tsubu*), or rye (*hadakamugi*). Rice (*kome* or *genmai*), buckwheat (*sobamugi*), and millet (*kibi*) are gluten-free. Tamari can be a good gluten-free alternative, as well.

The first time I ate at a Japanese restaurant, I distinctly remember the salad and wanting to drink the remaining dressing after I ate the greens, because it was so tasty.

Place in a blender:
1/8 cup of chopped onion
2 heaping teaspoons of chopped ginger
1 1/2 tablespoons of gluten-free miso
1/4 cup of rice vinegar
1 1/2 teaspoon of agave nectar
1/2 chopped carrot
1/8 teaspoon of crushed garlic
1/4 cup water
1 tablespoon of tomato paste or gluten-free ketchup
2 tablespoons of lemon or orange juice

Because of how robust this dressing tastes, it usually is served on a simple salad of greens, cucumber, tomato and scallions.

## Recipe: Appetizer—Miso Soup

(Serves 4)

(Refer to the last recipe for the directions of buying gluten-free miso. The key to keeping miso nutritious is to never heat it to a boil.)

Place in a sauce pan:
4 soup bowls of water
1/4 cup of grated onion
1/8 cup of chopped cilantro
1/2 teaspoon of crushed ginger
1/4 cup of fresh or frozen peas
1/4 cup of soft, gluten-free tofu cut in small cubes
salt to taste

(Optional: In Japan, instead of the cilantro, you could use 2 tablespoons of fish oil and one package of dried seaweed.) After the broth boils, reduce the heat to simmer, cover and let steep for 10 minutes. Take off of the heat.

With 1/2 cup of warm water, whisk 2 tablespoons of miso to create a thick liquid. Add this mixture to your broth just before serving.

To make this soup a meal, you can add:
Boiled, gluten-free soup noodles, sliced carrot, celery, bok choy, or snow peas.

# Recipe: Side Dish—Cold Szechwan Sesame Noodles

(Serves 4)

Boil 9 ounces of ziti, gluten-free pasta, first. Cook until the pasta is of desired tenderness. Immediately, drain in a colander and rinse with cold water. While in the colander, toss 2 tablespoons of either peanut or sesame oil into the pasta. Let the pasta sit at room temperature while you prepare the sauce and toppings.

Toppings
Chop in a separate bowl:
1/2 cup of thinly sliced lettuce
1 cup of long, thin slices of cucumber, removing the seeds from the center with a small spoon and cutting from top to bottom
1/2 cup of thinly sliced red and green pepper
1/2 cup of parboiled snow peas, cut down the center long wise
3 chopped scallions

Prepare sesame sauce:
In cast iron or nonstick skillet, slow roast 1/2 cup of raw sesame seeds with no oil in the pan. When the first seed pops, remove the pan from the heat. The seeds should look toasted.

Place seeds in food processor or use a mortar and pestle to crush:
Fold in 2 tablespoons of natural peanut butter
1 tablespoon tahini

In a separate sauce pan:
Boil 2 tablespoons of Sake or rice cooking wine
Melt in 3 tablespoons of brown sugar
When sugar dissolves, remove from heat.

# Gluten-Free, High-Protein, Vegetarian Cookbook

Whisk 2 tablespoons of gluten-free miso in 1/2 cup of warm water.

Mix together:
Sesame seed mixture;
Sake and sugar mixture; and
Miso
(Optional: You can also add to this mixture 1 teaspoon of chili paste for heat.)

Toss this sauce into the cool pasta. Serve pasta topped with chopped lettuce, cucumber, scallions, snow peas and peppers.

# Recipe: Main Course Protein— Teriyaki Tofu

(Serves 4)

Teriyaki is one of my favorite Japanese sauces. So, when I became a vegetarian, I sincerely missed having things dressed with this sauce. Though teriyaki tofu is not usually on a Japanese menu, you can usually request it.

The Prep:
*Teriyaki Sauce*:
Heat in a small sauce pan until sugar is dissolved:
3 tablespoons of tamari
2 tablespoons of sake or rice wine
2 teaspoons of light brown sugar

Marinate 10 ounces of sliced (not too thin) tofu in teriyaki sauce. After marinating, cover tofu slices with nutritional yeast and sesame seeds. In a baking dish coated with nonstick olive oil spray, bake tofu slices for 20 minutes on each side at 375°. The texture of the tofu is up to you. Personally, I like it a little chewier, so I let mine get brown and chewy.

15 minutes before you desire to serve your dish, make your stir fry, using the recipe from the Asian section at the back of this book; however, you will substitute one of Chinese sauces for the teriyaki sauce:

2 minutes before you serve, stir in the teriyaki sauce and prepared tofu. Cover and let steam together for 2-3 minutes.

Serve hot with a small serving of brown or jasmine rice.

# Recipe: Meal—Greenwich Village Favorite

(Serves 2)

In a small New York City restaurant, teeming with NYU students and locals, I discovered this meal, trying to live frugally and also remain a vegetarian.

Prepare:
Miso Carrot Dressing (in the Japanese section of this chapter)
2 servings of your favorite rice
A side salad with sprouts, tomato, cucumber, onion, and lettuce.

Either bake or fry a meat-free protein (tofu burger, veggie burger, Quorn™, or cut up Tofu Pups™). Whichever you choose, for extra flavor, top it with cheese.

Place a bed of the rice on each dish. On top of the rice, place your meatless protein. To the side of the rice, place the salad right on the plate. Then cover the entire dish with warm miso carrot dressing.

## ITALIAN DISHES

# Recipe: Appetizer—Agli a Olia Soup

(Serves 4)

I am Italian. When it comes to traditional favorites, you can always count me in. However, I try to only eat pasta once every other week. My dad used to make this soup on a cold, winter evening for a snack for his six kids. We would all sit around the table and eat 2 or 3 bowls each. The soup had so much heat, my inner ears would burn. That was a good thing.

Boil 10 cups of water in a large sauce pan.

In a frying pan, sauté 2 tablespoons of olive oil:
1 1/2 teaspoon of minced garlic
1/4 cup of chopped and diced sweet onion (Vidalia, if available)
1/2 stalk of chopped celery
1 chopped banana pepper (green will do in a pinch)

When onions become translucent, add:
1 teaspoon of frozen or store-bought basil in a jar or five fresh chopped basil leaves.
Dash of dried oregano
2 dashes of paprika
Salt and ground pepper to taste.
Add 1/4 cup of your boiling water to this sauté mixture and reduce heat to simmer. Cover with a lid.

When the 10 cups of water boils, add small, gluten-free noodles to the pot. Let the noodles cook until *al dente* (cooked, but still firm). Add the sautéed mixture to the pasta and boiling water. Don't drain the water from the noodles. We use this water to create the soup.

# Gluten-Free, High-Protein, Vegetarian Cookbook

The secret to this recipe is: you must use 1/4 cup of the juice from either pickled hot or pickled sweet banana peppers. This just doesn't taste like Dad's soup, unless you use the pickled pepper juice. If you don't have pickled peppers, 1/2 teaspoon of dill seasoning will give you the basic flavor.

For protein:
Add cubed, unbaked soft tofu.

# Recipe: Main Protein—Baked Italian-Style Tofu

(Serves 4)

You can do a lot of things with tofu. The baked texture—when you let it get crispy is quite good and can be substituted for chicken in a meal. Sometimes, after baking tofu, I'll rebread it and fry it in olive oil to give it a heartier, Italian texture and taste.

Slice 16 ounces of tofu into slabs 1/8-1/4" thick. (Remember: the thinner you slice the tofu, the tougher it gets, when baked.)

Marinate these slices for one hour in:
1/4 cup of Bragg's liquid aminos
1 teaspoon of chopped garlic
1 teaspoon of olive oil
1 teaspoon of onion salt
1 tablespoon of Balsamic vinegar

Mix dried ingredients well. (Hint: you can make more of this dried mixture than you need and store it in an air-tight container for use with other recipes.)

1/2 cup of nutritional yeast
1/2 cup of gluten-free breadcrumbs (Remember, you can make your own from stale and hard, gluten-free bread. Just leave it on the counter overnight. It will get hard enough to grate or food process into crumbs.)
1 teaspoon of garlic powder
1 teaspoon of onion salt
1 teaspoon of dried oregano
1 teaspoon of dried basil
1 teaspoon of dried parsley
1 teaspoon of dried dill
1/2 teaspoon of rosemary powder

# Gluten-Free, High-Protein, Vegetarian Cookbook

1 teaspoon of dried mustard
1/2 teaspoon of paprika
2 dashes of cayenne pepper
Crushed melange of pepper—to taste
1/2 teaspoon of salt

Drain marinade from tofu.

Thickly coat the tofu strips with the dried yeast ingredients from above. If you don't mind using egg, bind the ingredients together by first placing the tofu in an egg wash, before applying the dried ingredient mixture.

Bake 45-60 minutes on a greased cookie sheet at 400° until coating becomes crispy. Turn the tofu one time at 30 minutes.

Hint: Spray the top side of the tofu with olive oil cooking spray for an extra crispy texture. If you do this, you won't have to turn the tofu over.

# Recipe: Sauces—Fresh Tomato Sauce

(Serves 4)

Most of my older relatives never made fresh tomato sauce. My Italian relatives always cooked their sauce to a slow death, all day. This particular sauce has the traditional Italian taste, but with a lot less saturated fat. Feel free to omit the butter and wine, but know it will not taste quite as authentic.

In a large 4"-deep skillet, sauté:
2 teaspoons of chopped garlic
1 tablespoon of olive oil
Be careful not to burn the garlic.

When garlic turns light brown add:
1 16-ounce can of diced tomatoes
1 16-ounce can of crushed tomatoes
(Optional: You can add 4 cups of fresh tomato sauce instead of canned.)
(See preparing sauce from fresh tomatoes in "Other Important Cooking Facts" in Chapter Four.)

Add:
1/4 stick of butter or 1/4 cup of olive oil
1/8 cup of red or white wine
2 tablespoons of frozen basil or 1/2 cup chopped fresh basil
1/4 cup of chopped chives or scallions
1 tablespoon of chopped fresh or a dash of dried oregano
1 dash of rubbed thyme
1/4 cup of chopped fresh parsley
1/8 cup of Romano cheese
Crushed melange of peppers to taste

When the sauce begins to steam, reduce the heat to low and taste the sauce. If the tomatoes are too acidic or tart, add 1/4 teaspoon of baking soda. The top of the sauce will froth for a moment as the soda eats away the excess acid. This should rectify the acidy flavor completely.

# Gluten-Free, High-Protein, Vegetarian Cookbook

Now is the time you begin to taste the sauce. Because tomatoes never taste the same, you sometimes have to add a bit of something sugary or salty. If the sauce tastes as if it needs a bit of sweet, add a little agave nectar or sugar. If it tastes bland, add a bit of salt. Another option is to add sliced carrots for sweetness.

Other optional ingredients:
1 cup of chopped mushrooms
1/4 cup of sliced black olives

Let sauce come to a slow boil, then reduce to a simmer on the lowest heat for 30 minutes. Sometimes, I boil my water for the pasta at the same time I begin the prepartion of the sauce and both finish at the same time.

If you have more time, after the sauce comes to a boil, take it off of the heat completely and let it marinate with a lid on for two more hours, instead of letting it simmer.

# Recipe: Sauce—Sun-Dried Tomato Pesto

(Serves 4-6)

After preparing this recipe, you can place it in a plastic freezer bag, flatten it out with a rolling pin, and then freeze the leftovers to be used in other recipes. I enjoy stirring 1/8 cup of sun-dried tomato pesto into hummus. This recipe can also be used to cover a cream cheese ball for a great appetizer at a party. Just place the cheeseball covered with sun-dried tomato pesto in the middle of a decorative plate and arrange some gluten-free crackers around the side with a couple sprigs of fresh parsley, and you'll be the hit of the party!

Soak in 1 cup of boiling water, then cover with a lid:
12 sun-dried tomatoes

In 2 tablespoons of olive oil, brown:
2 heaping teaspoons of minced garlic
1/4 cup of pine nuts
(Optional: you can substitute the pine nuts for chopped walnuts or pistachios.)
When golden brown, let cool.

Remove sun-dried tomatoes from water, but save the water. Place the plump, hydrated tomatoes in a food processor with the garlic and nuts.

Add:
1/4 cup of fresh or frozen basil leaves
1/4 cup of Pecorino Romano cheese

To cut down on fat, you may use the water you saved from soaking the tomatoes to thin the mixture. Or, for a more traditional texture, use 1/8 cup of olive oil. Food process on pulse.

# Gluten-Free, High-Protein, Vegetarian Cookbook

Always use a heavier pasta with this sauce, so it does not break up when you toss in the sun-dried tomato pesto. We still don't have many gluten-free choices of heavier pastas, so just use ziti.

Boil the pasta to the desired texture. Drain the water from the pasta in a colander.

Toss 2-3 tablespoons of butter or 2 tablespoons of olive oil into the pasta while it's steaming. (To cut down on fat even more, use more of the water you saved from soaking the tomatoes, instead of the butter.)

Toss in half of the pesto mixture. This pesto is intense, so try the pasta with half of the mixture, first, then add more until it's just right for you.

Top this with more Romano cheese or nutritional yeast.

# Recipe: Sauce—Sweet Basil Pesto

(Serves 4)

Nothing says nouveau Italian more than pesto. You can grow sweet basil in most areas of the country during the sunny seasons. Just keep cutting away the flowers and the basil will continue to grow all season and not go to seed.

In a food processor or with a mortar and pestle combine:
1 cup of fresh basil leaves (about 20 leaves)
1/4 cup of pine nuts
2 heaping teaspoons of minced garlic
1/4 cup of Pecorino Romano cheese
Process on high until nuts are ground completely.

Always use a heavier pasta with this sauce, so it does not break up when you toss it. Ziti is fine. Boil the pasta to the desired texture. Drain the water from the pasta in a colander.

Toss 2-3 tablespoons of butter or 2 tablespoons of olive oil into the pasta while it's steaming.

Toss in half of the pesto mixture. This pesto is intense, so try the pasta with half of the pesto, first, then add more until it's just right for you.

Top this with more Romano cheese.

## Recipe: Main Course Protein— Italian Soysage and Fried Peppers

(Serves 4)

Sol Cuisine™ is one of the few companies that makes a vegetarian sausage patty without gluten, however it does contain soy. If you're sensitive to soy, avoid this recipe.

In a large skillet on medium heat, add:
2-3 tablespoons of olive oil
1 teaspoon of chopped garlic
1 whole sliced medium onion
3 to 4 peppers, a garden variety is nice, one yellow, one green, one banana, one red
1 package of Sol Cuisine™ sausage patties.

Sauté or fry entire mixture until onions are browned and translucent and peppers are toasty. Your entire house should smell amazing.

# Recipe: Quick Meal—Pizzazzing a Gluten-Free Pizza

(Serves 2)

Toppings always make the pizza. Typically, the gluten-free, pre-made pizzas are a little dry and not so flavorful. Here are some things you can do to make one better.

In 1 teaspoon of olive oil, sauté 1 teaspoon of minced garlic until it is light brown.
Add 1 teaspoon of chopped fresh or frozen basil

Before you put the pizza in the oven, top it with this mixture. Add some protein by cutting up some of your favorite veggie protein on the top.

Also, try the following options:
Add: 1/2 teaspoon of dried oregano
Add: some grated Romano cheese and some mozzarella cheese

Bake as required on package.

# Recipe: Hearty Soup—Pasta y Faziole

(Serves 4-6)

Some traditional Italians prefer to use this recipe with full strength tomato sauce and eat this as a meal on a plate with pasta. Personally, I like the soup version below.

In a skillet, sauté in 1 tablespoon of olive oil, until brown:
1/2 cup chopped onion
2 teaspoons of chopped garlic
(Optional: 1/4 cup of chopped banana pepper)

While you are sautéing:
Boil 6 cups of water in a sauce pan
Add 1 teaspoon of salt
When the water comes to a boil, add 1/2 cup of gluten-free soup noodles.
Let boil for 8 minutes on medium high, then turn down to simmer.

Add to boiling water:
1 16-ounce can of crushed tomatoes
Your sauté mixture from above
1/2 can of kidney beans
1 tablespoon of frozen sweet basil or 4 fresh leaves or 1 teaspoon of dried basil
1/8 cup of fresh, chopped parsley
1 pinch of dried oregano

Add salt and pepper to taste. Simmer for 15 minutes and serve topped with Romano or Parmesan cheese. If you are lactose intolerant, sprinkle nutritional yeast on the top.

# Recipe: Main Course—
# Cold Pasta Salad

(Serves 4)

Everytime I want to impress dinner guests with recipes that are quick and attractive, I prepare this pasta salad. It is a simple and wonderful summer dish, filled with fresh garden herbs and vegetables.

Prepare 8 ounces (a half-box) of gluten free ziti pasta.
After boiling, drain in a colander.
Run cold water over the pasta until it cools.
Place pasta in a large serving bowl.

Add:
2 cups parboiled broccoli cut into bite-sized pieces
8 ounces of sliced black olives
1 jar of marinated artichoke hearts (chopped)
(Optional: 4 ounces of cubed cheddar cheese)
(Optional: 4 ounces of cubed mozzarella cheese)
2 stalks of chopped celery, including celery leaves
1 cup of diced, ripe tomatoes (if out of season, use canned)
4 chopped scallions
1/2 cup of chopped green bell pepper
1/2 cup of yellow bell pepper

Add chopped herbs:
3 sprigs of fresh parsley leaves
4 basil leaves
2 sprigs of fresh dill or 1/2 teaspoon of dried dill
20 leaves of oregano, or 1 teaspoon of dried oregano

Hint: I have a pair of very good kitchen scissors that I use to cut herbs. I grab the entire handful of herbs in one hand, and snip with the other hand directly into the pan.

The Dressing:

# Gluten-Free, High-Protein, Vegetarian Cookbook

1/2 teaspoon of garlic powder
1/2 teaspoon of onion salt
1 teaspoon of dried mustard
3 tablespoons of raw, apple cider vinegar
1/2 cup of olive oil

(As an alternative: Make the salsa recipe and toss it into your vegetable salad, but exclude the diced or canned tomatoes from the original recipe. Especially in the summer, the lime juice, cilantro, and fresh tomatoes make for the perfect flavor to enhance any salad.)

Mix all of the ingredients with the cold pasta and let marinate in the refrigerator for an hour or more. The longer all the ingredients have a chance to merge, the better it tastes. This recipe lasts in your refrigerator for 3-4 days without going bad. (Depending on your taste, you may want to add a bit more vinegar or lime juice.)

# Recipe: Main Course Protein— Stuffed Bell Peppers

(Serves 4)

I love the taste of roasted peppers. This recipe uses the basic tofu burger from the American section of this chapter as a filling. Consider one thing when creating this recipe: you can either stuff the peppers from the top by coring them and taking out the centers, or you can simply cut the peppers in half, taking out the insides and stuffing the halves. You get more stuffing to pepper ratio the second way.

Mix up the tofu burger mixture.
Prepare red, yellow, or green bell peppers for stuffing as described above.
Stuff 4 whole or 8 half-peppers with the tofu mixture.
Place in a baking dish with, at least, 1/2 inch of water.
Pour 1/2 of a 16-ounce can of crushed tomatoes over the top.
Top peppers with a sprinkle of nutritional yeast or Romano cheese.

Add:
2 tablespoons of olive oil
1 tablespoon of dried basil or six chopped, fresh leaves
3 sprigs of chopped parsley leaves
Salt and pepper to taste
1 sliced, medium onion, strewn around the peppers
1 teaspoon of garlic salt, sprinkled on top

(Optional: Bake with added extras, such as, quartered new potatoes, whole carrots, or sliced celery. I enjoy a mixture of all of the above. The carrots, onion, and celery, also, give you the advantage of preparing an entire meal in one baking dish.)

## MEDITERRANEAN FARE

## Recipe: Appetizer—Lentil Soup
(Serves 4-6)

A dear friend grew up with a very traditional Greek mother, who showed her the way around the kitchen. My friend advised me about this recipe, which is simple and full of protein.

Soak 16 ounces of lentils in water for at least an hour.

Empty water and add 4-5 cups of fresh, purified water. The more water you use, the more soupy the texture.

Add to broth:
2 tablespoons of tamari
One grated medium-sized onion
1 stalk of chopped celery
2 sliced carrots
1/2 teaspoon of chopped garlic
Ground melange of pepper to taste
1/8 cup of olive oil
5 whole bay leaves (remove after cooking)
Salt to taste
Optional: 1 scant teaspoon of dried dill

After the soup comes to a boil, reduce the heat and let simmer for 45-60 minutes, or until the lentils become tender. The longer you cook the soup, the more the soup turns into the texture of refried beans.

Serve with a dollop of fresh, plain, organic yogurt, a dash of nutrional yeast, or a tablespoon of the Greek cucumber dressing, which follows.

# Recipe: Dressing—Cucumber Yogurt Dressing

(Serves 8)

This dressing is great over almost any Mediterranean dish. I enjoy it as a salad dressing, as well. Make the marinated, fried tofu and create your own Middle Eastern delight. Pick one of the gluten-free, vegetarian chicken substitutes, which would also be a great choice with this dressing.

Purée in blender:
1/4 cup of olive oil
1/2 teaspoon of chopped garlic
1/2 teaspoon of salt
1/4 cup of lemon juice
2 scallions
1 cup of yogurt
1 medium-sized cucumber, sliced in half, removing the seeds with a small spoon. Dispose of the seeds.

Pour the puréed mixture into a mixing bowl and add 1 cup of low-fat sour cream. Stir together to make a creamy dressing.

## Recipe: Side Dish—Tabouli

(Serves 4)

Tabouli is such a beautiful side dish. It looks delicious and tastes equally as good and fresh; however, it is traditionally made with bulgar wheat, which is in the no-gluten zone. Try this version of tabouli and let me know what you think.

Cook brown jasmine rice a little less than the directions say, so that it remains a bit crunchy. Drain excess water and let cool as you stir in one teaspoon of rose water (this is my special secret ingredient).

Add chopped herbs and vegetables:
One bunch of parsley tops—about 1 cup
1/8 cup of chopped mint leaves
4 diced and chopped scallions
1 large ripe tomato cut in small cubes
(Optional: 1/2 cup cubed cucumber without the seeds)

Dress salad with:
1/8 cup of lemon juice
1/8 cup of olive oil
Salt and pepper to taste

Mix salad and decide if you need to tweek this with a little more lemon juice, salt, or olive oil.

## Recipe: Protein Main Dish—Falafel

(Serves 4)

This recipe is a small diversion from the original, which included wheat. Most of this protein, however, is derived exactly from what gluten-free bread uses as its main ingredient—chickpea flour or ground garbanzo beans, which are the same thing.

In a large mixing bowl:
Soak one pound of garbanzo beans in cold water overnight.
The dark, bad beans will float to the top. Remove them and the water. Let dry. Food process the beans a little at a time in a heavy-duty processor until all beans are ground. Place in mixing bowl.

Separately, food process:
1 medium onion (slice it first so it processes quicker)
1 potato (slice it first so it processes quicker)
4 cloves of garlic

You should end up with a course mixture of the above ingredients, then add these herbs to your food processor:

1/2 cup of cilantro leaves
1 teaspoon of ground pepper
1 teaspoon of ground cumin
1 teaspoon of ground coriander
1 teaspoon of salt
1/2 teaspoon of paprika
2 teaspoons of lemon juice
1 tablespoon of olive oil
1 tablespoon of chickpea flour
2 teaspoons of baking soda

Add this mixture to your garbanzo meal.

# Gluten-Free, High-Protein, Vegetarian Cookbook

Form heavy batter into small balls and fry in hot oil 1/4 inch deep.

After frying, place the falafel on some paper towels to drain the excess fat, as you prepare the Tahini Sauce topping.

Tahini Sauce:
In blender mix thoroughly:
1 cup of sesame tahini
1/2 cup of purified water
1/2 cup of lemon juice
1 1/2 teaspoons of chopped garlic or 3 cloves of garlic
1/2 teaspoon of salt

Serve the falafel with the tahini dressing. Add some tabouli as a side dish. Hummus would also make a great combination on this plate.

Traditionally, falafel is put on pita bread with the tahini sauce. Try placing the falafel on a bed of saffron rice, if you need an extra carbohydrate. Then cover with the tahini sauce. I have also had the cucumber dressing on falafel and loved it.

# Recipe: Main Course Protein—Fried Marinated Greek Tofu

(Serves 4)

This is an answer to a marinated chicken substitute. If you slice the firm tofu in long strips and fry it for 10-12 minutes, the tofu becomes tough and chewy.

Cut 16 ounces of firm, gluten-free tofu into long strips.

In a sealed covered bowl, marinate tofu for, at least, one hour in:
3 tablespoons of Bragg's liquid aminos
2 tablespoons of Balsamic vinegar
1 teaspoon of garlic powder
1 teaspoon of onion powder
1 teaspoon of Montreal Steak Seasoning

Drain marinade from tofu before frying.

In skillet:
Preheat 1 tablespoon of olive oil.
Add:
Tofu strips
1 or 2 sliced green or red bell peppers, and
1 sliced medium-sized onion.

Fry mixture until tofu gets crispy brown and onions and peppers become soft and seared.

Serve over brown rice with the yogurt dressing or the tahini dressing from the falafel recipe.

## Recipe: 10-Minute Meal—Tofu Salad
(Serves 3)

If you have been wondering what cold tofu tastes like, this is a recipe that you may want to try. This recipe, in texture, is similar to egg salad and can be used on a sandwich or as a side, protein dish.

Crumble 4-6 ounces of firm tofu into a mixing bowl.

Mix in a separate bowl:
1 tablespoon of tahini
2 tablespoons of rice vinegar
1 tablespoon of gluten-free miso
(Optional: 1 dash of curry powder or 1 dash of rubbed thyme.)

Gently stir sauce into the crumbled tofu.

Add to mixture:
1/4 cup chopped black or green olives
1 chopped scallion
1/2 stalk of chopped celery

Stir the entire mixture gently with a fork. It should look like egg salad.

# CHINESE (ASIAN) CUISINE

## Recipe: Soup—Hot and Sour Soup

(Serves 4)

When I found out that traditional hot and sour soup was made with pork blood, I was horrified. Needless to say, I quickly ended my relationship with this Asian delight and set a course to develop a vegetarian version that would suit my Epicurean taste.

In a saucepan, boil:
1 cup of water

Add:
1 teaspoon of agave nectar or sugar and
6 dried shitake mushrooms.
Let this mixture soak for 15 minutes.
Remove and slice the mushrooms, making sure you save the water from soaking the mushrooms.

In a saucepan, add to the mushroom juice:
3 cups of water
6 sliced and hydrated shitake mushrooms
1/2 cup of sliced bamboo shoots
1 1/2 ounces of cubed tofu
1/4 cup sliced canned mushroom or fresh Monterey mushrooms
1 tablespoon of dried, black tree fungus

Season with:
2 tablespoons of tamari
1/4 cup of rice vinegar
1 teaspoon or more of hot chili paste
Salt and pepper to taste.

# Gluten-Free, High-Protein, Vegetarian Cookbook

Bring to a boil. Reduce heat and let cook on medium heat for ten more minutes.

To thicken soup, in separate bowl whisk:
1 tablespoon of xantham gum and
1/2 cup warm water.

Make the soup as thick as you want by slowly adding the xantham mixture until the soup is the desired thickness.

(Optional: whisk in hot soup, 3 egg whites or 1/2 cup of egg substitute)
(Optional: add 1/2 cup gluten-free soup noodles)

# Recipe: Soup—Vegetable-Tofu Soup

(Serves 4-6)

This recipe adds a simple herb broth to a high protein favorite with some fresh veggies. It's hearty, when you're in a pinch for an entire meal in one bowl.

Bring to a boil:

4-6 cups of water

1/4 grated medium-sized onion

1/2 teaspoon of chopped or crushed garlic

1 tablespoon of fresh or dried chopped rosemary

1/4 teaspoon of grated ginger

2 tablespoons of olive oil

1/4 teaspoon of chili paste—increase if you like heat

1 tablespoon of chopped parsley leaves

5-6 ounces of cubed, soft tofu

Salt to taste.

Add a small combination of the following vegetables or some of your own favorites:

1/2 cup of thinly sliced carrots

1/2 cup of diced celery

1 cup of bite-sized broccoli pieces

1/2 cup of snow peas

1/2 cup of oyster or canned mushrooms

1 cup of chopped boy choy

Cook with the vegetables on simmer for about 5-10 minutes extra or until the vegetables are at the texture you enjoy eating them. Serve topped with chopped scallions.

# Recipe: 10-Minute Meal— Egg Foo Yong

(Serves 2)

Every time I have shown my students how to make this dish, they cannot believe how simple and fast it is to make. Also, the presentation is beautiful. Egg Foo Yong is basically an omelet, so, if you do not eat eggs, avoid this recipe.

Prepare the sauce topping, first.
In a small sauce pan, boil:
1/2 cup of water
3 tablespoons of sake or rice cooking wine
1 teaspoon of agave nectar or brown unrefined sugar
1 tablespoon of tamari
1 dash of salt

When mixture comes to a boil, add:
1 teaspoon of xantham gum

Whisk to dissolve the xantham gum and turn off, covering to keep warm.

The Vegetables:
Sauté in one teaspoon of olive oil, 8 spears of asparagus. Cook for 2-3 minutes.

The omelet:
In a skillet, fry:
3 beaten eggs or 3/4 cup egg substitute in light cooking oil, not olive oil. When the entire bottom surface is golden brown, flip the egg over to cook the inside.

Place the cooked asparagus in the center of the egg and fold over.
Top the omelet with the sweet and sour sauce and chopped scallions.

# Recipe: Main Course—Stir-Fried Vegetables

(Serves 4)

Below, I explain how to create three different sauces to add to your stir-fry. Each sauce adds a different flavor for the vegetables. Beginning with the least intrusive of the recipes, the white sauce allows you to taste more of the natural flavors of the vegetables. The brown sauce definitely becomes bolder and richer. The garlic sauce, which is hot and tangy, is my personal favorite.

The Thickening Agent:
For all sauces, whisk 1 teaspoon of xantham gum or one tablespoon of Arrowroot into 1 cup of warm water.

Prepare the sauce you choose for your stir-fry first.

White Sauce:
Just add salt and white pepper to the thickening agent. Add this liquid to your vegetables. Cover with a lid and let simmer for 3 minutes, before serving.

Brown Sauce:
Combine in a bowl or cup:
2 tablespoons of tamari
1/2 teaspoon of agave nectar
3 dashes of white pepper
1/2 teaspoon of salt
1 tablespoon of sesame oil
After mixing thoroughly, stir into to your vegetables, 3 minutes before serving and cover with a lid.

Garlic Sauce:
Combine in a cup or bowl:
2 tablespoons of water from soaking 2 shitake mushrooms
2 tablespoon of tamari

# Gluten-Free, High-Protein, Vegetarian Cookbook

2 tablespoon of Bragg's Liquid aminos
1 or 2 teaspoons of chili paste
2 tablespoons of rice vinegar
1/2 teaspoon of salt

After mixing thoroughly, stir into to your vegetables, 3 minutes before serving. Cover with a lid and let the flavors mingle.

The Stir-fry:

Woks cook food at different temperatures, because the bottom of the wok gets the most heat and the sides are cooler. Vegetarians have no meat to cook, so a wok is fairly moot. Stir-fry all your vegetables at once, unless you like to brown onion and garlic first, then barely cook your broccoli and larger vegetables. I use a large deep skillet made for deep frying to stir-fry.

First, cut and dice your vegetables, ahead of time. Cutting the vegetables in different shapes and sizes makes the dish look more interesting. For example, you may want to cut some celery in small, bite-size pieces and some in long strips. With vegetables such as broccoli and cauliflower, cut approximately one-inch pieces, so the veggies don't break apart and cook too quickly.

In most stir-fries, use up to eight vegetables, but no more. However, we always start with the following:
Chopped pepper
Chopped onion
Minced garlic and
Minced ginger

Depending on the amount of stir fry you make, you need to adjust the amount of each of the latter to your personal taste.

Once the onion and garlic mixture begins to brown, add your protein. Let fry for another 2-3 minutes.

Protein choices:
Baked Tofu
Raw, firm tofu
Quorn cooking chunks
Your Favorite Meat Substitute
Egg

After 3 minutes, add the rest of your chopped vegetables.

Choose from the list below:
Zucchini
Bok Choy
Baby yellow squash
Asparagus
Green beans
Celery
Bamboo shoots
Mushrooms—oyster, portabella, shitake, or any exotic mushroom
Broccoli
Nappa—Chinese cabbage
Baby yellow corn
Cauliflower
Snow peas
Bean sprouts
Water chestnuts

The heat should be high enough to make a sizzling sound when the vegetables hit the oil—medium high. Stir them around for 3 minutes, letting them get toasty. Then add 1/4 cup of water and place a lid on the top for 1-2 minutes to let the vegetables steam.

Now season with one of the stir-fry sauces in the Chinese or Japanese section of this book. Again, cover and let the sauce permeate the taste of the stir-fry for 3 minutes.

# Recipe: Main Dish—Lomein Substitute

(Serves 4)

Lomein is a particular kind of Chinese noodle, slightly thicker and tougher in texture than most Italian noodles. However, all lomein is made with gluten, so we are going to substitute Thai, long, rice noodles—either bean thread or the thicker versions.

Prepare 4 servings of noodles according to the directions. (Most rice noodles are soaked, not boiled.)

Prepare the basic stir-fry recipe from the last section, but use only the following vegetables, after your initial garlic and onion mixture:
1 cup of sliced celery
1/2 cup of sliced mushrooms
1/4 cup of chopped scallion
1 cup of chopped nappa
1 cup of mung bean sprouts

After two minutes of stir-frying the basic ingredients with the above vegetables, add the noodles. Fry in the oil for 2-3 minutes.

If you want to add a 1/2 cup of the brown sauce, that is optional. Otherwise, just salt to taste.

(Optional: The original Thai recipe also uses a fried and scrambled egg with a couple of dashes of chili paste. The dish becomes almost like a Pad Thai.)

(Optional: You can also add chopped cashews or peanuts and a drizzle of lime, for a different taste.)

# Recipe: Main Course Protein—Kung Pao Tofu

(Serves 4)

You can use this hot and spicy peanut sauce to enhance a stir-fry or simply pour over baked or French fried tofu, which is the Chinese tradition. You can keep this sauce prepared in the refrigerator for about two weeks without it going bad.

Mix in blender:
1/4 cup of peanuts
1 heaping teaspoon of natural peanut butter or cashew butter
3/4 teaspoon of chili paste
1 teaspoon of chopped garlic
3 tablespoons of tamari
1 tablespoon of sesame oil
1 teaspoon of rice vinegar
2 heaping teaspoons of grated ginger (peel off the brown skin)
1/4 teaspoon of flaked red pepper
1/4 cup of water
1/2 teaspoon of arrowroot

Once you add this sauce to noodles, vegetables or your tofu, let it heat to warm, then serve.

## Other Health Tips

I have tried many different modalities of healing for the body. Each time I try something new and different, I am changed. Not every modality may be for me, but I certainly learn what may be good for someone else in the trying.

Becoming gluten free has changed my life and lifestyle. I'm more energetic, my muscles ache a lot less, my body fat has reduced considerably, and my stomach and IBS problems are almost completely gone.

The most important aspect about maintaining good health is learning to listen to your body. You can't expect to know what you need, if you have never learned to listen to your own personal needs. In my coaching practice, I have realized that the majority of overweight or morbidly obese clients have difficultly carving out time for themselves. They tend to be people-pleasers and garner all of their self-esteem from helping others.

Trust me on this one truth: If you don't take care of your own body first, you won't have a body with which to help anyone else!

Peace begins in meditation and with practice. Don't expect to get to nirvana overnight. I have spent my entire life practicing yoga and meditation and eating right, so that I can get to that blissful place outside of my body now and again to glean the power and energy I need for a healthy life.

My other self-help books, **Finding Authentic You, The Uncommon Gay Spiritual Warrior, Theoraphasz: God Speak in the Final Phase of Human Development,** and **The Protein-Powered Vegetarian**, will all help you on a path toward greater peace and developing the power you need to create a wonderful life.

But, if you don't learn to listen to your own body, you will never succeed in any kind of physical change, especially a habitual one. One of the most important facets of training the mind and body to listen to your highest good is to learn to control your breath. Each time you inhale, move your eyes to the right and count five or six beats to breathe in and the same count to exhale. As you exhale, move your eyes to the left.

The eyes dictate which side of the brain you use. So, when you move the eyes during meditation, you confuse the deductive mind enough to release it. This is a great trick during the day, if you get sidetracked and anxious. Just stop, breathe, and move your eyes from left to right like small erasers, until you begin to feel your mind slowly releasing your negative thoughts.

After about three minutes of breath work, then stop controlling your body and your breath completely. Sit or lie as still as you can and wait for your body to breathe on its own volition. As you do so, you, also, automatically get into the observer mind.

When you don't control your legs and let them feel as if they are disconnected from your mind, you automatically move into the observer side of the brain. Once there, you must sit in the silence between your breaths.

Keeping the mind silent is no easy feat. To stop your mind from chattering, imagine that everything that you hear in your mind translates to a picture in your mind. So, I hear myself thinking, "I have to get to the dentist tomorrow to get my teeth cleaned!" Instead of focusing on the whys and hows of that problem, I would try to create the clearest picture of what being at the dentist would look like on a movie screen in my mind.

The idea, here, is to take what is deductive—the internal thinking mind—and turn it into the inductive dreaming mind by substituting pictures for words. Seeing something manifest in your mind as a picture uses the subconscious mind. So, you automatically move back into meditation, simply by taking the words in your mind and changing them to pictures.

I think this is the best trick I have ever learned in my life, as it had taken me 15 years to understand just this much about meditation. So, hopefully, you can circumvent all of my years of learning in one easy lesson. Now, don't expect for meditation to be easy. Most people have to wrangle with their deductive mind a lot to get it to do what he or she asks. This is normal.

Don't be hard on yourself when you begin to practice meditation. Some neophytes begin with just five to ten minutes a day of silence. Of course, the most adept meditators will spend hours sometimes in a seated position, which at my age is an impossibility. My back just can't handle the lotus position with no back support for meditation, anymore. In fact, I can't remember when my back could stay seated that long. I always felt too uncomfortable to meditate when I tried doing it seated and on the floor. Get comfortable. Even if you fall asleep, your subconscious mind will remember all it needs to remember during the process.

### Waking Up

In the moments, just as your mind regains consciousness, is the time when you will receive most dispensations and communication from Spirit. I sometimes get very clear pictures of what I need to do as the next step toward changing my *current story* to something more awesome and powerful. For instance, one morning, I woke up with the idea that all of the work I had been doing in many facets of my life could fall under one heading: ***Finding Authentic You***. The moment was surreal and wonderful. I felt such peace in the understanding that my life would somehow change by asserting this information as a *brand* into my life.

As you can see, much of my life and business is based on the premise of finding your authentic self. This is my second cookbook. I have also written novels and self-help books and a blog with hundreds of discoveries concerning the meditation process: http://www.findingauthenticyou.com.

### Doing Your Part

I love the Buddhist theory that most of the human existence is considered a teaching time for us to let go of our basic instincts to crave, honor, and be controlled by the lust and greed of the human *pain body*. When we let go of the human nature, we have the opportunity to let our human vessel be filled with divine understanding. These principles are ones that will help the earth evolve into the Kingdom of God, instead of the kingdom of man.

We all need to do our part. But, as I said before, we can't even begin to *see* our part, unless we take time to observe our human condition—first, in ourselves. Then we must observe it in our lives and in the people around us.

Once you see that man is headed for destruction, given his reptilian fears and desires, we can understand that our lives here as humans are dependent on the discovery of something far greater than the best job, a fair mate, and financial stability. When you recognize that your path and life is contingent upon the rest of humanity moving forward toward unity and love, you make a more concerted effort to evolve into a better human.

### Be Prepared for Change

Who said that the best made plans are laid to waste? The Master Jesus taught us in the scriptures that a good builder starts with a plan. I believe that a blueprint of your future is a good first step, even with good eating habits. But, that blueprint must come from Spirit; otherwise, you will keep falling, tripping, and turning around until you're facing in the direction Spirit needs you to be moving. I get this now, after many missteps. So, I acquiesce to change as soon as it happens. I follow change with meditation to get my spirit and mind in line with God's plans.

I believe that the blueprint we create, inevitably will be half with Spirit and half with our human mind. We can't help but to involve the very part of our human mind that had gotten us this far in our lives. Our deductive, thinking mind plays a very important role in getting us to our spiritual goals. But, it must play the *subordinate* role; otherwise, we will travel in circles around Mount Olive to get to the promises of God.

Meditation is a deep human sleep, while the spirit stays awake and conscious, so that your mind can sense the spirit interrupting the human process, the subtle neural pathways, and less-than-subtle torment of other's opinions.

**Walking the Path Toward Change**

Webster says that change means: *to make or transform completely.* Change isn't something that happens overnight. Think about the journey of the caterpillar. It crawls on its belly for awhile, skirmishing about in the dirt, before it ever climbs a tree and spins its cocoon. Whenever it moves into silence, the transformation begins. It metabolically changes every cell to become a flying creature. The metaphor of the butterfly is an amazing way to consider change. If you just ponder it for awhile, you will never be the same.

Once, about ten years ago, a very large, green, speckled caterpillar climbed up behind the gutter of my house and spun a huge web there. I watched it for a long while as its cocoon appeared to weather with the seasons. After a long time, on a spiritual high, I arrived home after teaching a yoga class. The butterfly had eaten its way halfway out of the cocoon. The fledgling, winged creature was as large as a hummingbird. It crawled up the side of the house and began to spread its beautifully colored wings. I had never seen a butterfly so large and exotic in my entire life. I felt privileged just to be witnessing such an event as this.

It fluttered its wings a few times, but seemed to be afraid to take off. It was then that I decided to help it out. I put my finger out and it hopped onto my hand. I gazed down at it with wonder and delight, walking to my front yard. I talked to it as I would a child, "Come on! You can do it. Try to fly!"

The butterfly seemed to understand. It flapped and flapped, and jumped a bit. Then, I said, "Ready?" And I whisked it up toward a tree branch. Instead of perching on the branch, it simply flew away, sailing higher than most birds. I never saw a butterfly like that again, even in a butterfly sanctuary I visited in the Caribbean.

**Personal Challenges**

You can't decide that you want to change, even your diet, without something inhibiting you. Life is rife with people and critics who mock authentic change. No one believes a person can make true change, until it actually happens. So, the only person you must try to change for is yourself. Believe me, if you decide to change for someone else, you might as well give up now.

If a client comes to my office and says he wants to quit smoking because his wife doesn't like the smell, I tell him to go home and come back when he wants to quit. The client may be successful in quitting for a reason, such as one of his children coming down with cancer. But, most times, a simple desire from a mate isn't enough to sustain real change.

Change must come from the core of your being. When a person wants to lose weight, he or she must have a very good reason, or you will succumb to the many ways you can cheat on a diet. Trust me on this one. If you had read my book ***Finding Authentic You—Book One***, you will know that I went through about four different diets before I ever discovered what it would take for me to personally lose weight.

My story was that I had always been skinny. People would make fun of me and tell me to gain weight. I look at old pictures of myself and I seem emaciated in some of my younger pictures. As I passed thirty years old, weight sort of snuck up on me. One day at the YMCA, I got a fat content test. I remember the day as if it were yesterday. The woman who administered the test took a metal gismo that looked similar to pliers and squeezed a piece of fat from my back, which I had no idea I had. Who looks at his back? I had never.

At that time, I had 18% body fat. I immediately went home and noticed that I had developed small, but ample, love handles. I was mortified! *My God,* I thought, *how in the world did this happen?* I immediately got back on a more rigorous exercise regimen and lost the love handles.

But as fifty began to creep up on me, the weight was harder and harder to lose. I would eat perfectly until the evening, then I would use every excuse in the book to eat something that wasn't on my diet. My excuse was always, "Well, I'm a thin person. I could use a little weight!" These were the same words I had heard half of my life. I used them to inhibit my own diet, every time.

When I discovered that I looked more attractive with more weight on, getting into shape became even harder. Suddenly, my fat content was in the upper 20s. Honestly, I'm not sure how that happened. I do yoga almost every day. I eat very healthy food. But, sometimes, I just binge on too much of one thing.

Finally, after much trial and error, I found that gluten was the cause of the weight gain and some of my stomach problems, too. So, after going on a gluten-free diet for about two months, I lost 19 pounds. I did step up my yoga to everyday, whether I felt as if I wanted to exercise or not. After three months my body fat reduced from 29.9% to 13.9%.

Keeping the weight off for six months has taken diligence. I know that one of the main reasons I want to keep it off is because I'm moving to Florida, where my shirt will probably off more than it is on. So, it's no wonder that most Floridians spend a lot of time in the gym.

You don't often go to South Beach and see heavy people. People on the beach in skimpy swimsuits are usually the prettiest of the pretty. They flaunt their muscles and are proud of their physiques, as they should be. But, one thing is for certain, they train hard and eat right to stay healthy, especially if they want to maintain a good figure as they age.

**Prosperous Thinking**

When the world was in its toddler phaze, nomads dragged around their belongings in the dessert. I'm certain, that one day, someone discovered that if he took some logs and rolled them underneath his belongings, it was a great deal easier to move. Eventually, someone thought of making the logs into a wheel. Most modern day manufacturing results from this one invention.

Can you imagine when the first person decided to carve a log into a wheel, what his sister, brothers and friends said. I'm sure he heard people say, "What on earth are you doing? Can't you see that pulling our belongings around is better than any new-fangled way you could think up?" Most people resist change until it becomes common place.

Can you remember the first time you heard about Facebook? I remember I got about twenty invites before I decided to even look at it. Once I joined, I couldn't get off of it. Now, instead of saying, "Hey, email me that," we say, "Just Facebook me." Just a decade years ago, Facebook didn't even exist. Now, people can't seem to exist without products such as LinkedIn, Twitter, and cell phones. Can you imagine what a day would be like without your computer? I can't. My entire day revolves around something that didn't even exist when I was a child.

I showed my 82-year-old mother things on my computer and talk to Siri on my Iphone, and she just is aghast with disbelief. I asked her one day, "When you were a child, did you ever imagine asking your phone to send a message to someone across the ocean?" She shook her head. "Not in a million years, did I think that." And my mother was a forward thinker.

Change isn't something that just happens. Change is an organic movement forward, just as Spirit continually moves forward to create more and more universes, beyond our own.

## Gluten-Free, High-Protein, Vegetarian Cookbook

So, to be connected with spirit, we must learn the movement of change; otherwise, we will be left behind. Change is inevitable. Change is in everything you see, everything you do, and everything you can imagine. The only thing you cannot change is change.

Learning to be on a gluten-free diet and being healthier is part of your new, abundant life. You simply can't make change without the belief that you deserve all that you have, all that you will receive, and the reciprocity from all that you have given in the past. I actually do feel completely different as a result of rethinking my life and going gluten free. As I have made room for health, prosperity, and purged the negativity from my life—including bad food; I feel, now, that I'm on the road to abundant living.

# *Author's Bio*

Bo Sebastian has been a Vegetarian Chef to vegetarian dignitaries and a teacher of the vegetarian way to chefs around the globe. His innovative book: *The Protein-Powered Vegetarian* helped many people add important vegetable protein to their diets, in a time when vegetarians had little to choose from in the form of protein. Now, Chef Bo comes back with important information and recipes for today's growing need to understand Gluten-Free Cooking.

Bo has also had five well-known works published including his most recent self-help guide, *Finding Authentic You: 7 Steps to Effective Change*. Also, *Your Gay Friend's Guide to Understanding Men*, a collaborative novel, *Summer in Mossy Creek* with Bell Bridge Books and BelleBooks Publishers, and *The Protein-Powered Vegetarian*. He also has a fitness DVD: *Boga Fitness*, merging Yoga with core strength and fitness exercises.

Bo has written five novels: *The Leaving Cellar, Billy Ray's Secret, Marlene and the Religiously Insane, Fatal Virtues,* and a young reader's novel, *Willa Divine, The Princess of Dixon Country.*

Bo is the author of the world famous blog: FindingAuthenticYou.com and proudly wears the hat of renowned, spiritual-, life-, and health-coach in south Florida. For more information visit BoSebastian.com.

Printed in Great Britain
by Amazon